The Ultimate Frozen Drink Directory

The only frozen drink book you will ever need

Includes 775 Classic & New Recipes

Written and Compiled by:

Dennis A. Wildberger

Introduction

Mixing drinks is both an art and a science. The art is easy: create a pleasant-tasting, attractive-looking cocktail in a clean glass with the proper garnish. The science is harder.

The science of cocktail making involves many things. It is knowing the exact ingredients for the drink you are building. Knowing the exact measurements of the aforementioned ingredients. Knowing which glass is the proper glass for each specific drink. What is the proper garnish? Etcetera, etcetera.

It is impossible for one human being to physically remember the details of every drink recipe ever created. Who would want to? It is for that reason, in part, that I created the "The Ultimate Frozen Drin k Directory".

Now, I'm not claiming that within these pages you will find the recipe for every frozen drink ever invented. However, what you will find here are the recipes for 775 of the most popular, classic, and creative frozen beverages ever consumed.

Many of the recipes in this book come from twenty-five years of personal experience working behind the bars of countless pubs, cafes, nightclubs, and restaurants. Very early on, I became a student of the bar industry. I strove to learn everything I could about the craft of bartending. I wanted to learn how to make every cocktail imaginable. I bought the few drink books that were available, studied them, and was disappointed every time. Not only was each bartender's guide short on recipes, they were all just duplicates of each other, and for the most part, out-of-date.

I decided that if I wanted to learn the recipes, I had to go to the source: my customers and my fellow bartenders. If someone requested a drink that I didn't know how to make, I was not shy about asking (in a way that didn't make me look like an idiot) "do you know what's in that?" Many a night I came home from the job with a pocketful of recipes that I had hurriedly scribbled on cocktail napkins as the patron rattled off the ingredients for a drink I'd never heard of.

Most of these recipes come courtesy of bartenders from all corners of the world. Some of these drinks are house specialties, some of these are bartender specialties. Most of these are just good drinks. One thing is for sure in any case: I thank each and every one of you who took the time to write down the ingredients for all of those cocktails you've given, sent, or emailed me over the years. Without you, the bartending profession would not be the same.

Within these pages, you will find the proper recipes for tons of frozen drinks. More importantly, you will find them in alphabetical order.

I have done my best to stay true to the exact ingredients in each recipe. If the original drink (as it was relayed to me) called for, let's say, Midori Melon Liqueur, the recipe, as it is written in this book, reads that way. However, it is up to you, the mixologist, to decide for yourself whether you will use any substitutions.

This manual was created for every bartender, waitress, home mixologist, and liquor industry professional. It is meant to replace all of the other drink reference books you have on your shelf or under your bar. I trust it will do the trick. Enjoy!

Supplies You Will Need

When creating the perfect frozen drink, it is important that you have at your disposal certain items to make the job easier. Here is a list of some of the crucial and optional accessories you may need:

Blender - A good-quality blender is essential for making these delicious frozen drinks. Normally, the blender cup will hold up to 64 ounces, so you can make double or triple batches at the same time. I prefer a heavy-duty blender with a stainless steel cup that has a tight-fitting plastic or rubber lid.

Ice Cream Scoop - A good ice cream scoop with a stainless steel of plastic handle is a must have when making most frozen drinks. Necessary for sherberts and ice creams.

Bar Spoon - A long-handled, stainless steel spoon will allow you to easily guide the frozen mixture out of the blender and into the glass.

Ice Scoop - A small ice scoop is necessary to help you to quickly fill your blender with the required amount of ice cubes.

Jigger Measure - A jigger measure is a convenient way to accurately measure the exact ingredients in your drinks. Made of stainless steel or plastic, one side of a normal jigger holds 1/2 ounce, the other side holds one full ounce.

Can Opener - Also know as a "church key", this item is needed for opening juice cans and such.

Speed Pourers (optional) - All of your frequently used liquor bottles should be topped with a speed pourer. They allow you to accurately create a precise stream of liquid without going through the hassle of removing the cap from the bottle. Speed pourers should fit snuggly into the bottle.

Measured Pourer (optional) - Similar to the speed pourer, a measured pourer will allow only a certain amount of fluid to pass through it before it automatically cuts off. These are good as a timesaving method, and for helping you measure exact amounts, but can occasionally be irritating. Measured pourers are commonly available in one ounce and 1 1/4 ounce pours.

Funnel (optional) - A small funnel should always be kept on hand. It is a invaluable tool in transferring liquids from one container to another without spillage.

Glass Rimmer (optional) - A nice accessory to have. It will allow you to quickly "rim" your glass (as required) with salt or another condiment. Professional glass rimmers commonly have three separate compartments: one to hold salt, one to hold sugar, and the other that has a round sponge insert that can be moistened with fruit juice. They fold up nicely for storage.

Storage Bottles (optional) - Also known as "store-&-pour" containers, these plastic bottles are excellent for refrigerating juices. Since it is not advised to store juices in the can after they are opened (the can will impart a "tinny" flavor), transferring the juice to a storage bottle is recommended. They have a speed pour-type top, are color-coded to match the juice (red for tomato, etc.), and are dishwasher safe.

Glassware

Glassware is an extremely important part of building the perfect cocktail. Presentation is everything. Glassware varies from establishment to establishment, and in most cases, your only choice is the glass that the boss provides.

When choosing a glass for a cocktail, always use the glass that is appropriate for that particular drink: martinis in a martini glass, brandies in a snifter, etc.

Throughout this book, a suggestion is usually included with each recipe as to the appropriate glass to use. Generally, if a specific glass is not suggested, the drink should be served in a standard 8 to 10 ounce highball glass. For example, if the directions in a recipe state "shake all ingredients with ice", or "stir all ingredients with ice", it normally means that the drink is served in a highball glass. However, this is also dependent upon the measure of the ingredients in the drink. If the recipe calls for 3 1/2 ounces of liquid ingredients or more, and no suggestion is made as to which glass to use, a highball glass is in order. However, if the recipe calls for 3 1/2 ounces of liquid ingredients or less, and no suggestion is made as to which glass to use, a lowball glass (or your particular version of a lowball glass) should be used.

When you pick up a glass to make a drink, the very first thing you should do is to give the glass the "once over". What that means is that you should hold the glass up to a light source so that you can see all of the way through it. By doing this, you make sure that the glass is absolutely clean, dry, and that there are no nicks or cracks in it. It should be common sense to never serve a cocktail in a dirty or cracked glass. If the glass is dirty, or has major water spots on it, put it aside to be washed, and select another glass. If it is cracked or nicked, even if the crack appears ever so slight, throw the glass away! The risk is never worth it when that glass could break in a patron's hand or cut their lip.

After washing your glassware, whatever method you use, the glasses should be allowed to air-dry. Sometimes you see in those old Western movies, the bartender drying the glasses with a bar towel. This should not be done. Towels and cloths have a tendency to leave specks of lint on a glass, causing the ruin of many a fine drink. Simply placing the
wet glassware on a drying rack or mat is sufficient, as long as the glass is raised off of the surface enough to allow air to circulate to the inside of the glass.

Here are some basic glassware types:

Shot Glass - (1 - 1 1/2 oz.) - for single liquor shots and small shooters as called for.

Large Shot Glass - (1 1/2 - 2 oz.) - for double shots and shooters as called for.

Pony or Cordial - (1 - 1 1/4 oz.) - for single shot cordials and liqueurs, shooters, and layered drink

Cocktail Glass - (4 - 6 oz.) - for drinks stirred or shaken with ice and strained, for an "up" cocktail.

Martini Glass - (5 - 10 oz., sometimes larger) - for certain "up" drinks, as called for.

Sour Glass - (4 - 5 oz.) - for certain "up" drinks, as called for.

Lowball or Shooter - (4 - 6 oz.) - for single or double liquors or liqueurs served "on the rocks", cocktails served "on the rocks" with less than 3 1/2 ozs. of total ingredients, and most shooters.

Highball Glass - (7 1/2 - 10 oz.) - for cocktails served "on the rocks" with more than 3 1/2 ozs. of total ingredients.

Collins Glass - (8 - 10 oz.) - for certain cocktails served "on the rocks" as called for.

Old-Fashioned - (4 - 6 oz.) - for single or double liquors or liqueurs served "on the rocks", cocktails served "on

Hurricane Glass - (8 - 16 oz., sometimes larger) - for larger cocktails served "on the rocks", and for certain frozen drinks as called for.

Sherry Glass - (3 - 4 oz.) - for single servings of sherries and Port wines.

Champagne Glass - (4 - 6 oz.) - for champagne and sparkling wines, and certain cocktails as called for.

Champagne Flute - (5 - 6 oz.) - for champagne and sparkling wines, and certain cocktails as called for.

White Wine Glass - (5 - 7 oz.) - for white wine service, and certain cocktails as called for.

Red Wine Glass - (6 1/2 - 10 1/2 oz., sometimes larger) - for red wine service, and certain cocktails calling for a large wine glass.

Brandy Snifter - (5 - 14 oz., sometimes larger) - for brandy and cognac service, and certain cocktails as called for

Irish Coffee Mug - (8 -10 oz.) - for most hot drinks, and certain other cocktails as called for.

Espresso Cup - (2 - 4 oz.) - for certain hot drinks, as called for.

Pilsner Glass - (9 - 13 oz.) - for draft beer, and certain cocktails as called for.

Beer Mug - (10 - 14 oz.) - for draft beer, and certain cocktails as called for.

Pint Glass - (16 oz.) - for draft beer, and certain larger cocktails as called for.

Building the Perfect Frozen Drink

Creating a perfect frozen drink is easy. First, find the recipe that you want to make. Next, gather the ingredients and supplies that you will need. Finally, follow these step-by-step procedures:

1. Into an empty blender cup, add proper amount of ice, as required in recipe. (If recipe doesn't call for ice, skip this step.)
2. Add recipe ingredients to the blender cup, one ingredient at a time.
3. Cover blender cup tightly with blender cap.
4. Holding blender cap firmly in place, turn blender on high.
5. Process cocktail for 15 to 30 seconds, or until drink is smooth.
6. Turn off blender. Remove cap.
7. Slowly pour cocktail into the proper glass, using a long-handled bar spoon to guide the drink into the glass without spilling.
8. Add proper garnish, as required.
9. Insert into the cocktail a long drinking straw or two sip sticks.

Garnishes

Garnishing a frozen drink is the crowning step that adds attractiveness and a last bit of flavor. It is often forgotten, but is still an important ingredient.

When making garnishes, always use fresh products. There is no faster way to ruin a perfectly good drink than by dropping a rotten piece of fruit into it. Besides, you are taking all of the time to create a perfect frozen drink, shouldn't the garnish you put on top be perfect also?

When cutting fruit, here are some tips you should always remember:
1. Always use a very clean cutting board that is used only for fruit. Never use a cutting board that has been used to cut raw meat.
2. Always use a clean, sharp fruit knife.
3. Make sure that your hands are clean and dry as possible. Wet hands could cause your knife to slip, creating an accident.
4. The container used to store the finished garnishes should be washed and dried before adding new fruit.

Lemons and Limes
The outside of lemons should be bright yellow, firm to the touch, and have a slightly oily feel to the skin. When sliced open, the pulp should be juicy and plump with no brown or dry-looking spots. They should have a nice, fresh, pleasing aroma.

Limes should be a medium to dark green with no visible brown spots on the skin. When squeezed slightly, they should have a firm but not hard feel to them. When cut, the pulp, like the lemon, should be juicy without any dry spots.

Fruit Garnishes

Throughout this book, certain recipes call for a fruit slice, a fruit wedge, or a fruit wheel. Here are the instructions for cutting these. Use these instructions for lemons, limes, or oranges.

Slices

1. Chose a clean, fresh piece of fruit. Wash and dry fruit, if necessary.
2. Place the piece of fruit on a clean cutting board.
3. Using a clean, sharp fruit knife, cut 1/2 inch off of each end of the fruit.
4. Turning the fruit longways, slice completely through the fruit, so that you have two halves.
5. Place one-half of the fruit on the cutting board, cut side up.
6. Make a 1/4 inch deep cut down the center of the length of the fruit half (this is done so that the finished slice will sit nicely on the rim of a glass).
7. Turn the fruit half over on the cutting board so that the cut side is face down.
8. Starting at one of the cut ends, slice the fruit into 1/4 inch slices. When this is done, you should have several half-moon shaped slices that have a nice fan-like appearance from the cross-section of the fruit.
9. Repeat steps 5 through 8 on the other half of the fruit.
10. Place the finished slices in a plastic or glass container, cover and refrigerate.

Wheels

1. Chose a clean, fresh piece of fruit. Wash and dry fruit, if necessary.
2. Place the piece of fruit on a clean cutting board.
3. Using a clean, sharp fruit knife, cut 1/2 inch off of each end of the fruit.
4. Turn the fruit longways. Carefully make a 1/2 inch cut through the skin, going slightly into the pulp (this is done so that the finished wheel will sit nicely on the rim of a glass).
5. Starting at one of the cut ends, slice the fruit into 1/4 inch slices. When you are finished, you should have several fruit wheels that are a cross-section of the fruit.
6. Place the finished wheels in a plastic or glass container, cover and refrigerate.

Wedges

1. Chose a clean, fresh piece of fruit. Wash and dry fruit, if necessary.
2. Place the piece of fruit on a clean cutting board.
3. Using a clean, sharp fruit knife, cut 1/2 inch off of each end of the fruit.
4. Turning the fruit longways, slice completely through the fruit, so that you have two halves.
5. Place one of the halves on the cutting board, cut side up..
6. Cut the fruit half longways into three equal sections, starting at the center of the piece of fruit and angling your knife out, making pie-shaped wedges (if you are using a larger piece of fruit, cut the fruit into four equal sections).
7. Make a 1/2 inch cross-cut through the center of each wedge (this is done so that the finished wedge will sit nicely on the rim of a glass).
8. Repeat steps 5, 6 and 7 on the other half of the fruit.
9. Place the finished wedges in a plastic or glass container, cover and refrigerate.

Cherries

Cocktail cherries, or sometimes known as Maraschino cherries, are a common garnish.

Commercially available in jars that range from 8 ounces to gallon-size, cherries are artificially-colored bright red (green cocktail cherries are also available), artificially flavored, and packed in a super-sweet sugar syrup. They are available with stems attached, and without stems.

When is recipe calls for a cherry, it is suggested that the cherry be speared with a fruit pick, and rested on top of the drink. This makes it easier for the drink consumer to remove the garnish without having to dig their fingers into the cocktail.
Fruit picks come in many shapes, sizes, and colors. Miniature bamboo skewers and plastic sword-shaped picks are common.

Orange and Cherry "Flags"
Many recipes call for an orange slice and cherry garnish. A fancy way to achieve this is by spending a few extra minutes to prepare "flags". Here are the steps to make "flags":
1. Make orange slices (See "Slices").
2. Place a cocktail cherry on the center of an orange slice.
3. Using one hand, fold the ends of the orange slice up and around the cherry.
4. Using your other hand, skewer the garnish with a fruit pick, starting at one end of the orange slice, going through the cherry, and exiting at the other end of the orange slice.
5. Place the finished flags in a plastic or glass container, cover and refrigerate.

Whipped Cream
Many recipes call for a whipped cream topping. If you like, you can take the time to make your own by whipping cold, heavy cream with a little bit of sugar. This is time consuming and labor intensive.

For toppings on frozen drinks, I recommend that you use a good-quality, real cream, canned product. Many brands are available in the supermarket, store in the refrigerator for a good while, and when dispensed on top of a frozen drink, make a nice presentation.

Rimming
A few recipes in this book require a rimmed glass. Rimming is simply moistening the rim of a cocktail glass with a liquid, and dipping the rim into sugar, salt or other condiment. It is easy to accomplish, and can be done very quickly. Commercial glass rimmers (See "Rimmers" in the Supplies section) do make the job easier, but are not necessary. If you don't have a glass rimmer, pour your salt, sugar, or condiment onto a paper or ceramic plate that is wide enough to accommodate the rim of the glass. Here are the steps to take to rim a glass:
1. Choose the proper glass for the drink you are making.
2. Using a fruit wedge or slice, moisten the rim of the glass by running the pulp of the fruit around the edge of the glass.
3. Gently dip the rim of the glass into the sugar, salt, or spice (as required).
4. Set the glass upright, and allow the rim to dry for a few seconds.

"Finishing" The Cocktail
Sip sticks and drinking straws are the finishing touch of any frozen drink. Sip sticks are normally thin, plastic, 5-inch long straws available in assorted colors. A frozen drink should always be finished with a drinking straw or two sip sticks.

Abbot's Delight
2 oz. Frangelico
½ of a Ripe Banana
2 oz. Pineapple Juice
2 dashes of Bitters

Combine all ingredients in a blender with a scoop of ice. Process until smooth. Garnish with a pineapple chunk.

Absolut Reese's
1 ½ oz. Absolut Vodka
¾ oz. Light Rum
2 scoops Reese's Peanut Butter Cup Ice Cream

Combine all ingredients in a blender. Process until smooth.

Al Capone
1 oz. Absolut Vodka
½ oz. Campari
1 oz. Orange Juice
1 oz. Pina Colada Mix
1 tsp. Sugar

Combine all ingredients in a blender with a scoop of ice. Process until smooth.

Alaskan Polar Bear Heater
1 oz. Brandy
1 oz. Gin
1 oz. Light Rum
1 oz. Dry Vermouth
1 oz. Vodka

Combine all ingredients in a blender with a scoop of ice. Process until smooth.

Alien Abduction
1 oz. Melon Liqueur
1 oz. Cointreau
1 oz. Peach Schnapps
1 oz. Kiwi Juice

Combine all ingredients in a blender with a scoop of ice. Process until smooth.

All American Daiquiri Part 1
¾ oz. Light Rum
1 ½ oz. Sour Mix
½ oz. Blue Curacao

Combine all ingredients in a blender with a scoop of ice. Process until smooth.
In a hurricane glass, pour in Part 1, then fill with Part 2. Top with whipped cream and a cherry.

All American Daiquiri Part 2
¾ oz. Light Rum
2 oz. Strawberry Liqueur
½ oz. Grenadine

Combine all ingredients in a blender with a scoop of ice. Process until smooth.

Almond Amaretto Freeze
2 oz. Amaretto
1 oz. Cream
½ cup Sliced Almonds
2 scoops Vanilla Ice Cream

Combine all ingredients in a blender. Process until smooth.

Almond Banana Frost
1 ½ oz. Amaretto di Saronno
¾ oz. Light Rum
½ oz. Light Creme de Cacao
½ of a Ripe Banana
½ oz. Coco Lopez
2 tsp. Vanilla Yogurt

Combine all ingredients in a blender with a scoop of ice. Process until smooth. Garnish

Almond Chi Chi
1 oz. Creme de Noyeaux
2 oz. Vodka
3 oz. Coco Lopez
3 oz. Pineapple Juice
½ oz. Grenadine

Combine all ingredients in a blender with a scoop of ice. Process until smooth.

Almond Colada
1 ½ oz. Amaretto
¾ oz. Vodka
2 oz. Coco Lopez
1 tbs. Chocolate Syrup

Combine all ingredients in a blender with a scoop of ice. Process until smooth.

Almond Joy
2 oz. Dark Creme de Cacao
1 oz. Pina Colada Mix
1 oz. Cream
1 scoop Vanilla Ice Cream

Combine all ingredients in a blender. Process until smooth.

Almond Joy Mud Pie
2 oz. Dark Creme de Cacao
1 oz. Cream
1 Almond Joy Candy Bar
½ cup Sliced Almonds
1 scoop Vanilla Ice Cream

Combine all ingredients in a blender. Process until smooth.

Almond Joyous
1 ½ oz. Amaretto
1 ½ oz. Dark Creme de Cacao
1 oz. Cream
1 oz. Coco Lopez
2 scoops Vanilla Ice Cream

Combine all ingredients in a blender. Process until smooth. Garnish with a cinnamon stick.

Almond Mochaccino
¾ oz. Amaretto
¾ oz. Kahlua
1 ½ oz. Cold Cappuccino

Combine all ingredients in a blender with a scoop of ice. Process until smooth.

Almond Mud Slide
2 oz. Dark Creme de Cacao
1 oz. Cream
2 Oreo Cookies
½ cup Sliced Almonds
1 scoop Vanilla Ice Cream

Combine all ingredients in a blender. Process until smooth.

Almond Velvet Hammer
1 oz. Kahlua
1 oz. Dark Creme de Cacao
1 oz. Cream
½ cup Sliced Almonds
1 scoop Vanilla Ice Cream

Combine all ingredients in a blender. Process until smooth.

Aloha Berry
1 oz. Amaretto
1 oz. Black Raspberry Liqueur
2 oz. Pina Colada Mix

Combine all ingredients in a blender with a scoop of ice. Process until smooth.

Alotta Colada
1 ¼ oz. Pina Colada Schnapps
1 oz. Cream of Coconut
1 oz. Pineapple Juice
3 oz. Cream

Combine all ingredients in a blender with a scoop of ice. Process until smooth. Garnish with a pineapple slice.

Amaretto Chi Chi
1 oz. Vodka
1 oz. Amaretto
1 oz. Cherry Juice
1 oz. Pina Colada Mix
½ oz. Orange Juice

Combine all ingredients in a blender with a scoop of ice. Process until smooth.

Amaretto Colada
1 ½ oz. Amaretto
1 oz. Rum
2 oz. Pina Colada Mix

Combine all ingredients in a blender with a scoop of ice. Process until smooth. Garnish with a cherry.

Amaretto Daiquiri
1 oz. Amaretto
1 oz. Rum
2 oz. Sour Mix

Shake all ingredients with ice or combine all ingredients in a blender with a scoop of ice and process until smooth.

Amaretto Ecstasy
¾ oz. Amaretto
¾ oz. Dark Creme de Cacao
2 oz. Cream
½ cup Frozen Strawberries

Combine all ingredients in a blender with a ½ scoop of ice. Process until smooth. Garnish with a fresh strawberry.

Amaretto Freeze
1 oz. Amaretto
2 scoops Vanilla Ice Cream

Combine all ingredients in a blender. Process until smooth. Garnish with a cherry.

Amaretto Mudslide
1 oz. Amaretto
1 oz. Kahlua
1 oz. Baileys Irish Cream
1 scoop Vanilla Ice Cream

Combine all ingredients in a blender with ½ scoop of crushed ice. Process until smooth.

Amaretto Pina Colada
1 oz. Amaretto
1 oz. Rum
1 ½ oz. Pina Colada Mix
½ oz. Pineapple Juice

Combine all ingredients in a blender with a scoop of ice. Process until smooth. Garnish with a cherry.

Amaretto Rose
1 ½ oz. Amaretto
½ oz. Lime Juice
¼ oz. Sour Mix
2 oz. Fresh Strawberries

Combine all ingredients in a blender with a scoop of ice. Process until smooth.

Amoreous
1 ½ oz. Amaretto di Amore
4 oz. Strawberry Ice Cream

Combine all ingredients in a blender. Process until smooth. Garnish with a fresh strawberry.

Angelico
2 oz. Frangelico
2 scoops Vanilla Ice Cream

Combine all ingredients in a blender. Process until smooth. Top with whipped cream and a cherry.

Angostura Sundae
1 oz. Gold Rum
½ tsp. Bitters
2 scoops Vanilla Ice Cream

Combine all ingredients in a blender. Process until smooth. Serve in a champagne glass.

Antifreeze
1 oz. Blue Curacao
1 oz. Spearmint Schnapps
1 oz. 7-Up

Combine all ingredients in a blender with a scoop of ice. Process until smooth.

Apfel Brownie
1 ½ oz. Schoenauer Apfel Liqueur
½ oz. Mozart Chocolate Liqueur
1 oz. Cream

Combine all ingredients in a blender with ½ scoop ice. Process until smooth. Top with a few crushed walnuts.

Appalachian Special
2 oz. Light Rum
2 oz. Pineapple Juice
2 Slices Canned Pineapple

Combine all ingredients in a blender with a scoop of ice. Process until smooth.

Apple Annie
1 oz. Goldschlager
¼ oz. Dark Creme de Cacao
¼ oz. Courvoisier VS
½ oz. Apple Schnapps
1 scoop Vanilla Ice Cream

Combine all ingredients in a blender. Process until smooth. Garnish with a cinnamon stick and an apple slice.

Apple Colada
2 oz. Apple Schnapps
1 oz. Coco Lopez
1 oz. Cream

Combine all ingredients in a blender with a scoop of ice. Process until smooth. Garnish with an apple slice and a cherry.

Apple Daiquiri
1 ½ oz. Light Rum
½ oz. Apple Juice
½ oz. Lime Juice
1 tsp. Sugar

Combine all ingredients in a blender with ½ scoop of ice. Process until smooth.

Apple Granny Crisp
1 oz. Apple Schnapps
½ oz. Brandy
½ oz. Baileys Irish Cream
1 scoop Vanilla Ice Cream
1 Graham Cracker

Combine all ingredients in a
blender. Process until smooth.
Top with whipped cream and
a sprinkle of nutmeg.

Apple Hummer
1 ½ oz. Apple Schnapps
1 oz. Rum
1 scoop Vanilla Ice Cream

Combine all ingredients in a
blender. Process until smooth.

Apple Ice
1 oz. Gold Rum
1 oz. Orange Juice
¼ oz. Grenadine
¼ oz. Sour Mix
½ of a Cored Apple

Combine all ingredients in a
blender with a scoop of ice.
Process until smooth. Top
with whipped cream.

Apple Pie Ala Mode
¾ oz. Captain Morgan Spiced
Rum
½ oz. Apple Schnapps
2 oz. Apple Juice
2 tbs. Apple Pie Filling
1 oz. Coco Lopez
1 oz. Cream

Combine all ingredients in a
blender with a scoop of ice.
Process until smooth. Garnish
with an apple slice.

Apple Pina Colada
1 oz. Rum
1 oz. Apple Schnapps
1 oz. Pina Colada Mix
½ oz. Pineapple Juice

Combine all ingredients in a
blender with a scoop of ice.
Process until smooth.

Apple River Inner Tube
1 oz. Brandy
1 oz. Dark Creme de Cacao
1 scoop Vanilla Ice Cream

Combine all ingredients in a
blender. Process until smooth.
Garnish with an apple ring.

Apple Sauce
1 oz. Captain Morgan Spiced
Rum
3 oz. Apple Sauce
4 oz. Sour Mix
¼ oz. Triple Sec

Combine all ingredients in a
blender with a scoop of ice.
Process until smooth.

Apricot Brandy Slush
1 oz. Apricot Brandy
½ oz. Vodka
1 oz. Amaretto
1 oz. Orange Juice
1 oz. Apricot Nectar
2 oz. Lemonade

Combine all ingredients in a
blender with a scoop of ice.
Process until smooth. Top
with a dash of Bacardi 151
Rum.

Apricot Cream Dream
1 oz. Apricot Brandy
2 oz. Apricot Nectar
2 oz. Cream

Combine all ingredients in a
blender with a scoop of ice.
Process until smooth. Pour
into a large wine glass. Fill
with chilled champagne.

Apricot Cream Spritz
1 oz. Apricot Schnapps
1 oz. Cream
1 scoop Vanilla Ice Cream

Combine all ingredients in a
blender. Process until smooth.
Top with 1 oz. chilled
champagne.

Apricot Elixir
1 oz. Apricot Brandy
½ oz. Captain Morgan Spiced
Rum
2 oz. Cream

Combine all ingredients in a
blender with a scoop of ice.
Process until smooth.

Aquavit Freeze
3 oz. Aquavit
2 oz. Lime Juice
1 Egg White
Dash of Kirschwasser
1 tbs. Sugar

Combine all ingredients in a
blender with a scoop of ice.
Process until smooth. Garnish
with a lime wheel.

Atomic Shake
1 oz. Baileys Irish Cream
1 oz. Kahlua
½ oz. Vodka
1 oz. Cream
1 tsp. Sugar
1 scoop Vanilla Ice Cream

Combine all ingredients in a blender. Process until smooth.

Awesome Tropical Passion
1 ¼ oz. Melon Liqueur
1 ¼ oz. Strawberry Schnapps
1 ¼ oz. Creme de Banana

Combine all ingredients in a blender with a scoop of ice. Process until smooth. Garnish with an orange slice and a cherry.

B.B.C.
1 ½ oz. Bacardi Light Rum
1 ½ oz. Baileys Irish Cream
1 whole Ripe Banana
¼ oz. Coco Lopez

Combine all ingredients in a blender with a scoop of ice. Process until smooth.

B-52 Shake
1 oz. Kahlua
1 oz. Grand Marnier
1 oz. Baileys Irish Cream
1 scoop Vanilla Ice Cream

Combine all ingredients in a blender. Process until smooth.

Baby Jane
½ oz. Baileys Irish Cream
½ oz. Vodka
½ oz. Butterscotch Schnapps
½ oz. Grenadine
2 scoops Vanilla Ice Cream
2 Oreo Cookies

Combine all ingredients in a blender. Process until smooth. Garnish with a cherry.

Bailey de Cacao
1 oz. Vodka
1 oz. Baileys Irish Cream
½ oz. Dark Creme de Cacao
1 ¼ oz. Cream

Combine all ingredients in a blender with a scoop of ice. Process until smooth. Top with a drizzle of chocolate syrup.

Baileys Banana Colada
1 oz. Baileys Irish Cream
½ oz. Creme de Banana
½ oz. Dark Rum
3 oz. Pina Colada Mix
1 whole Ripe Banana

Combine all ingredients in a blender with a scoop of ice. Process until smooth.

Baileys Blizzard
¾ oz. Baileys Irish Cream
¾ oz. Brandy
¾ oz. Peppermint Schnapps
1 scoop Vanilla Ice Cream

Combine all ingredients in a blender. Process until smooth.

Baileys Iced Cappuccino
2 oz. Baileys Irish Cream
5 oz. Double Strength Coffee
1 oz. Cream
2 tsp. Sugar

Combine all ingredients in a blender with a scoop of ice. Process until smooth. Top with whipped cream and a sprinkle of cinnamon.

Banana Barbados
¾ oz. Mount Gay Rum
¾ oz. Myer's Dark Rum
½ oz. Creme de Banana
¼ oz. Sour Mix
2 scoops Vanilla Ice Cream

Combine all ingredients in a blender. Process until smooth. Top with a dash of Myer's Dark Rum.

Banana Boat
1 ½ oz. Tequila
½ oz. Creme de Banana
1 oz. Lime Juice

Combine all ingredients in a blender with a scoop of ice. Process until smooth.

Banana Bomb
2 oz. 99 Bananas
1 oz. Cream
¼ oz. Chocolate Syrup
1 scoop Vanilla Ice Cream

Combine all ingredients in a blender. Process until smooth.

Banana Colada
1 ½ oz. Rum
2 oz. Coco Lopez
1 Medium Banana
1 tsp. Lemon Juice

Combine all ingredients in a
blender with a scoop of ice.
Process until smooth.

Banana Daiquiri
1 ½ oz. Rum
½ of a Ripe Banana
½ oz. Sour Mix
1 tsp. Sugar

Combine all ingredients in a
blender with a scoop of ice.
Process until smooth.

Banana Di Amore
1 oz. Amaretto
1 oz. Creme de Banana
2 oz. Orange Juice
1 oz. Sour Mix

Combine all ingredients in a
blender with a scoop of ice.
Process until smooth. Garnish
with an orange slice and a
banana slice.

Banana Dream
1 ½ oz. Rum
1 oz. 99 Bananas
2 oz. Orange Juice
1 scoop Vanilla Ice Cream

Combine all ingredients in a
blender. Process until smooth.
Top with whipped cream.

Banana Fantastic
1 oz. Creme de Banana
½ oz. Light Creme de Cacao
½ oz. Vodka
1 oz. Cream
Dash of Galliano

Combine all ingredients in a
blender with a scoop of ice.
Process until smooth.

Banana Foster
1 ½ oz. Captain Morgan
Spiced Rum
½ oz. Creme de Banana
1 whole Ripe Banana
1 scoop Vanilla Ice Cream

Combine all ingredients in a
blender. Process until smooth.
Top with whipped cream and
a sprinkle of cinnamon.

Banana Mama
1 oz. Rum
¼ oz. Grenadine
3 oz. Pina Colada Mix
½ of a Ripe Banana

Combine all ingredients in a
blender with a scoop of ice.
Process until smooth.

Banana Piz
2 oz. Coffee Liqueur
1 oz. Light Rum
¼ oz. Cold Coffee
1 oz. Coco Lopez
1 whole Ripe Banana

Combine all ingredients in a
blender with a scoop of ice.
Process until smooth.

Banana Republic
2 oz. Light Rum
2 oz. Mango Juice
½ oz. Pineapple Juice
1 whole Ripe Banana
1 Pineapple Slice

Combine all ingredients in a
blender with a scoop of ice.
Process until smooth.
Fill with 2 oz. ginger ale.
Garnish with a cherry.

Banana Rum Frappe
2 oz. Light Rum
1 oz. Creme de Banana
2 oz. Orange Juice
½ oz. Triple Sec

Combine all ingredients in a
blender with a scoop of ice.
Process until smooth.

Banana Sipsop
1 ½ oz. Dark Rum
1 ½ oz. Cream
Dash of Grenadine
½ oz. Coco Lopez
1 Ripe Banana
Pinch of Ground Nutmeg

Combine all ingredients in a
blender with a scoop of ice.
Process until smooth.

Banana Split
1 ½ oz. Creme de Banana
1 ½ oz. Strawberry Liqueur
1 oz. Dark Creme de Cacao
1 scoop Vanilla Ice Cream
½ of a Ripe Banana
6 Strawberries

Combine all ingredients in a
blender. Process until smooth.
Top with whipped cream.

Banana Tree
1 oz. Creme de Banana
½ oz. Light Creme de Cacao
½ oz. Galliano
½ of a Ripe Banana
1 scoop Vanilla Ice Cream
4 Drops Vanilla Extract

Combine all ingredients in a
blender with ½ scoop of ice.
Process until smooth. Garnish
with a banana slice.

Banana Whirl
¾ oz. White Sambuca
¾ oz. Light Rum
1 oz. Lime Juice
½ of a Ripe Banana
½ tsp. Sugar

Combine all ingredients in a
blender with a scoop of ice.
Process until smooth. Garnish
with a slice of banana.

Bananaccino
¾ oz. Creme de Banana
¾ oz. Kahlua
1 ½ oz. Cold Cappuccino

Combine all ingredients in a
blender with a scoop of ice.
Process until smooth.

Bananas Barbados
1 oz. Mount Gay Rum
½ oz. Myer's Dark Rum
½ oz. Creme de Banana
2 oz. Sour Mix
1 Ripe Banana

Combine all ingredients in a
blender with a scoop of ice.
Process until smooth. Float ½
oz. Myer's Dark Rum on top.

Bananas Over You
½ oz. Creme de Banana
½ oz. Light Creme de Cacao
½ oz. Frangelico
2 oz. Cream
1 Ripe Banana
1 scoop Vanilla Ice Cream

Combine all ingredients in a
blender. Process until smooth.

Banilla Boat
1 oz. B&B
½ oz. Creme de Banana
1 scoop Vanilla Ice Cream
Dash of Nassau Royale
Liqueur

Combine all ingredients in a
blender. Process until smooth.
Garnish with a banana slice
and a filbert nut.

Barnamint Bailey
1 oz. Baileys Irish Cream
1 oz. Peppermint Schnapps
1 scoop Vanilla Ice Cream
2 Oreo Cookies

Combine all ingredients in a
blender. Process until smooth.

Barney's Revenge
1 oz. Vodka
1 oz. Blue Curacao
¾ oz. Apricot Brandy
½ oz. Raspberry Syrup

Combine all ingredients in a
blender with a scoop of ice.
Process until smooth.

Batidas
2 oz. Cachaca
2 oz. Strawberry Puree
1 oz. Sweetened Condensed
Milk
1 oz. Simple Syrup

Combine all ingredients in a
blender with a scoop of ice.
Process until smooth.

Bavarian Bliss
1 oz. Buttershots Schnapps
½ oz. Creme de Almond
1 scoop Vanilla Ice Cream

Combine all ingredients in a
blender. Process until smooth.
Top with whipped cream.

Bay City Bomber
½ oz. Vodka
½ oz. Rum
½ oz. Tequila, Gin
½ oz. Triple Sec
½ oz. Orange Juice
½ oz. Pineapple Juice
½ oz. Sour Mix

Combine all ingredients in a
blender with a scoop of ice.
Process until smooth. Float ¼
oz. Bacardi 151 Rum on top.
Garnish with an orange slice
and a cherry.

Beach Bum's Cooler
1 ¼ oz. Baileys Irish Cream
¼ oz. Creme de Banana
¾ oz. Rum
1 ½ oz. Pina Colada Mix
¼ of a Ripe Banana
1 scoop Vanilla Ice Cream

Combine all ingredients in a
blender. Process until smooth.
Garnish with a pineapple
slice.

Beachside
1 ½ oz. Melon Liqueur
1 oz. Light Rum
2 oz. Coco Lopez
6 Strawberries

Combine all ingredients in a blender with a scoop of ice. Process until smooth.

Beer Margarita
1 ½ oz. Tequila
1 ½ oz. Draft Beer
2 oz. Limeade

Combine all ingredients in a blender with a scoop of ice. Process until smooth. Pour into a salt-rimmed margarita glass.

Beer Shake
8 oz. Foster's Lager
2 scoops Mint Chocolate Chip Ice Cream

Combine both ingredients in a blender. Process until smooth.

Beerman Blend
2 oz. Tequila
2 scoops Orange Sherbet
3 oz. Cola

Combine all ingredients in a blender. Process until smooth.

Berkley
3 oz. Light Rum
1 oz. Brandy
1 oz. Passion Fruit Juice

Combine all ingredients in a blender with a scoop of ice. Process until smooth.

Berried Pleasure
1 oz. Strawberry Schnapps
1 oz. Amaretto
1 oz. Light Creme de Cacao
1 scoop Vanilla Ice Cream

Combine all ingredients in a blender. Process until smooth.

Berries 'N' Cream
½ oz. Captain Morgan Spiced Rum
¾ oz. Wilderberry Schnapps
3 oz. Strawberry Syrup
1 oz. Fresh Raspberries
2 oz. Cream

Combine all ingredients in a blender with a scoop of ice. Process until smooth. Garnish with fresh blueberries or strawberries.

Berryetto
1 oz. Rum
1 oz. Amaretto
4 oz. Fresh or Frozen Strawberries
1 scoop Vanilla Ice Cream

Combine all ingredients in a blender. Process until smooth. Garnish with a fresh strawberry.

Big Blue Sky
½ oz. Light Rum
½ oz. Blue Curacao
½ oz. Coco Lopez
2 oz. Pineapple Juice

Combine all ingredients in a blender with a scoop of ice. Process until smooth.

Big Chill
1 ½ oz. Dark Rum
1 oz. Pineapple Juice
1 oz. Orange Juice
1 oz. Cranberry Juice
1 oz. Coco Lopez

Combine all ingredients in a blender with a scoop of ice. Process until smooth. Garnish with a pineapple wedge and a cherry.

Black Colada
1 oz. Dark Rum
1 ½ oz. Coco Lopez
½ oz. Pineapple Juice

Combine all ingredients in a blender with a scoop of ice. Process until smooth. Garnish with an orange slice and a cherry.

Blackberry Bomber
1 ¼ oz. 99 Blackberries
1 ¼ oz. Chambord
1 ½ cups Fresh Strawberries
1 oz. Orange Juice

Combine all ingredients in a blender with a scoop of ice. Process until smooth. Float ¼ oz. Bacardi 151 Rum on top.

Blackberry Fruit Cream
1 ¼ oz. Blackberry Brandy
1 oz. Captain Morgan Spiced Rum
2 oz. Cranberry Juice
1 scoop Vanilla Ice Cream

Combine all ingredients in a blender. Process until smooth.

Blast from the Past
1 oz. Malibu Rum
1 oz. Smirnoff Vodka
1 oz. Jägermeister
1 scoop Strawberry Ice Cream

Combine all ingredients in a
blender with ½ scoop of ice.
Process until smooth. Garnish
with a cherry.

Bleeding Heart
½ oz. Maui Red Schnapps
½ oz. Maui Blue Schnapps
½ oz. Maui Tropical Schnapps
½ oz. Vodka
½ oz. Cranberry Juice
½ oz. Sour Mix

Combine all ingredients in a
blender with a scoop of ice.
Process until smooth. Top
with whipped cream.

Blended Comfort
1 oz. Southern Comfort
2 oz. Bourbon
1 oz. Orange Juice
¾ oz. Dry Vermouth
¼ oz. Sour Mix
½ of a Fresh Peach

Combine all ingredients in a
blender with a scoop of ice.
Process until smooth.

Blizzard
¾ oz. Baileys Irish Cream
¾ oz. Brandy
¾ oz. Kahlua
½ oz. Myer's Dark Rum
1 scoop Vanilla Ice Cream

Combine all ingredients in a
blender. Process until smooth.
Top with a nutmeg sprinkle.

Bloody Alligator
1 oz. Midori Melon Liqueur
¾ oz. Malibu Rum
½ oz. Lime Juice
¼ oz. Sour Mix
3 oz. Fresh Strawberries

Combine all ingredients in a
blender with a scoop of ice.
Process until smooth.

Bloody Patriot Eyes
2 oz. Vodka
2 oz. Pineapple Juice
1 ½ oz. Coco Lopez

Combine all ingredients in a
blender with a scoop of ice.
Process until smooth. Pour
into two separate shooter
glasses. Float ¼ oz. Parfait
Amour on top of each.

Bloody Pineapple
1 oz. Finlandia Pineapple
Vodka
½ oz. Blue Curacao
1 oz. Pineapple Juice
1 tsp. Sugar

Combine all ingredients in a
blender with a scoop of ice.
Process until smooth. Pour
into a shooter glass. Top with
¼ oz. Grenadine.

Blue Cloud
1 oz. Amaretto
½ oz. Blue Curacao
2 scoops Vanilla Ice Cream

Combine all ingredients in a
blender. Process until smooth.
Top with whipped cream and
a cherry.

Blue Colada
1 oz. Blue Curacao
2 oz. Light Rum
1 ½ oz. Coco Lopez
3 oz. Pineapple Juice

Combine all ingredients in a
blender with a scoop of ice.
Process until smooth.

Blue Daiquiri
1 ½ oz. Light Rum
1 ½ oz. Fresh Lemon Juice
1 oz. Blue Curacao
2 oz. Simple Syrup

Combine all ingredients in a
blender with a scoop of ice.
Process until smooth.

Blue Hawaiian
1 oz. Light Rum
1 oz. Blue Curacao
2 oz. Pineapple Juice
1 oz. Coco Lopez

Combine all ingredients in a
blender with a scoop of ice.
Process until smooth. Garnish
with a pineapple slice and a
cherry.

Blue Mango
1 oz. Blue Curacao
1 oz. Vodka
2 oz. Orange Juice
2 oz. Mango Puree

Combine all ingredients in a
blender with a scoop of ice.
Process until smooth. Top
with whipped cream and a
drizzle of Blue Curacao.

Blue Movie
½ oz. White Sambuca
¼ oz. Creme de Cassis
¼ oz. Blue Curacao
1 oz. Cream
½ of an Egg White

Combine all ingredients in a blender with ½ scoop of ice. Process until smooth. Pour into a large martini glass.

Blue Popsicle
1 ½ oz. Blueberry Schnapps
1 oz. Blue Curacao
1 oz. Triple Sec
1 ½ oz. Sour Mix

Combine all ingredients in a blender with a scoop of ice. Process until smooth.

Blue Sky
1 oz. Light Rum
1 oz. Blue Curacao
1 oz. Coco Lopez
4 oz. Pineapple Juice

Combine all ingredients in a blender with a scoop of ice. Process until smooth.

Blue Sky Colada
2 oz. Malibu Rum
1 oz. Blue Curacao
1 oz. Creme de Banana
1 scoop Vanilla Ice Cream

Combine all ingredients in a blender. Process until smooth. Garnish with a cherry.

Blue Sky Margarita
2 oz. Cuervo Gold Tequila
2 oz. Sour Mix
1 oz. Lime Juice
1 oz. Blue Cream Nehi Cola

Combine all ingredients in a blender with a scoop of ice. Process until smooth.

Blue Velvet
1 oz. Chambord
1 oz. Melon Liqueur
1 scoop Vanilla Ice Cream

Combine all ingredients in a blender with a scoop of ice. Process until smooth. Top with whipped cream and a dash of Blue Curacao.

Blue Voodoo
¾ oz. Rum
¾ oz. Blue Curacao
1 oz. Pina Colada Mix
1 scoop Vanilla Ice Cream

Combine all ingredients in a blender. Process until smooth.

Blueberry Cheesecake
1 ½ oz. Frangelico
1 ½ oz. Chambord
3 oz. Cream

Combine all ingredients in a blender with a scoop of ice. Process until smooth.

Blushin' Russian
¾ oz. Vodka
1 oz. Coffee Liqueur
1 scoop Vanilla Ice Cream
4 Strawberries

Combine all ingredients in a blender. Process until smooth. Garnish with a chocolate covered strawberry.

Blushing Bride
2 oz. White Sambuca
2 oz. Sloe Gin
Dash of Lime Juice
1 Egg White

Combine all ingredients in a blender with no ice. Process until smooth and frothy. Serve in a chilled martini glass.

Bourbon Slush
1 ½ oz. Bourbon
1 oz. Lemonade
1 oz. Orange Juice
2 oz. Unsweetened Iced Tea
1 tsp. Sugar

Combine all ingredients in a blender with a scoop of ice. Process until smooth. Garnish with a slice of lemon.

Brain Freeze
2 oz. Light Rum
2 oz. Vodka
Dash of Triple Sec
Dash of Strawberry Juice
2 oz. Tropicana Twister

Combine all ingredients in a blender with a scoop of ice. Process until smooth. Top with a splash of 7-Up.

Brandy Venetian
1 ½ oz. Brandy
1 oz. Frangelico
3 oz. Club Soda
1 scoop Vanilla Ice Cream
4 oz. Canned Peaches

Combine all ingredients in a blender. Process until smooth. Garnish with a slice of peach and a fresh mint leaf.

Brass Fiddle
2 oz. Peach Schnapps
¾ oz. Jack Daniel's
2 oz. Pineapple Juice
1 oz. Orange Juice

Combine all ingredients in a blender with a scoop of ice. Process until smooth. Top with a dash of grenadine, and swirl down into drink with a straw.

Brazilian Blast
½ oz. Frangelico
½ oz. Brandy
½ oz. Dark Creme de Cacao
½ oz. Rum
1 oz. Cream
1 scoop Vanilla Ice Cream

Combine all ingredients in a blender. Process until smooth. Top with whipped cream.

Brown Lady
1 oz. Coffee Liqueur
1 oz. Baileys Irish Cream
1 oz. Vodka
1 oz. Coco Lopez

Combine all ingredients in a blender with a scoop of ice. Process until smooth. Garnish with a pineapple chunk.

Buenos Dias
1 oz. Vodka
3 oz. Champagne
2 oz. Cranberry Juice
2 oz. Coco Lopez

Combine all ingredients in a blender with a scoop of ice. Process until smooth.

Bunky Punch
1 ½ oz. Vodka
1 oz. Melon Liqueur
1 oz. Peach Schnapps
1 ½ oz. Cranberry Juice
2 oz. Orange Juice
½ oz. Grape Juice

Combine all ingredients in a blender with a scoop of ice. Process until smooth. Garnish

Bushwacker
1 oz. Malibu Rum
1 oz. Bacardi Light Rum
1 oz. Kahlua
1 oz. Light Creme de Cacao
1 oz. Baileys Irish Cream
1 oz. Coco Lopez

Combine all ingredients in a blender with a scoop of ice. Process until smooth. Top with

Butt Munch
2 oz. Brandy
1 oz. Coffee Liqueur
1 oz. Cream
½ tsp. Ground Cinnamon

Combine all ingredients in a blender with a scoop of ice. Process until smooth. Top with whipped cream and a sprinkle of ground cinnamon.

Butter Blizzard
¾ oz. Captain Morgan Spiced Rum
¾ oz. Butterscotch Schnapps
2 oz. Cream
1 scoop Vanilla Ice Cream
1 Butterfinger Candy Bar

Combine all ingredients in a blender. Process until smooth. Top with whipped cream and some crushed Butterfingers.

Butterscotch Dream
½ oz. Butterscotch Schnapps
½ oz. Godiva Chocolate Liqueur
¼ oz. Cinnamon Schnapps
1 scoop Vanilla Ice Cream

Combine all ingredients in a blender. Process until smooth. Top with whipped cream and broken pieces of a toffee candy bar.

Butterscotch Hop
¾ oz. Butterscotch Schnapps
¾ oz. Kahlua
1 oz. Cream
1 scoop Vanilla Ice Cream

Combine all ingredients in a blender. Process until smooth.

Butterscotch Sundae
¾ oz. Kahlua
¾ oz. Butterscotch Schnapps
1 scoop Vanilla Ice Cream
1 Oreo Cookie

Combine all ingredients in a blender. Process until smooth. Top with whipped cream.

Butterscotch Twist
1 oz. Butterscotch Schnapps
1 ½ oz. Jack Daniel's
1 tbs. Sugar
2 scoops Vanilla Ice Cream
1 raw Egg

Combine all ingredients in a
blender with ½ scoop of ice.
Process until smooth.

C.M. Spiceberry
1 ¼ oz. Captain Morgan
Spiced Rum
3 oz. Fresh Strawberries
1 oz. Coco Lopez

Combine all ingredients in a
blender with a scoop of ice.
Process until smooth.

Cactus Colada
1 ¼ oz. Tequila
¾ oz. Melon Liqueur
1 oz. Orange Juice
1 oz. Pineapple Juice
2 oz. Coco Lopez
½ oz. Grenadine

Combine all ingredients in a
blender with a scoop of ice.
Process until smooth. Garnish

Caesar Makes Sense
1 ½ oz. Triple Sec
2 oz. Orange Juice
2 scoops Vanilla Ice Cream
Dash of Grenadine

Combine all ingredients in a
blender. Process until smooth.
Garnish with an orange slice.

Cafe Azteca
1 oz. Kahlua
1 oz. Tequila
1 tsp. Instant Coffee
1 scoop Vanilla Ice Cream

Combine all ingredients in a
blender. Process until smooth.

Cajun Cooler
1 ½ oz. Praline Liqueur
1 ½ oz. Light Creme de Cacao
1 scoop Vanilla Ice Cream

Combine all ingredients in a
blender. Process until smooth.

Calypso Cappuccino
¾ oz. Tia Maria
¾ oz. Dark Rum
1 ½ oz. Cold Cappuccino

Combine all ingredients in a
blender with a scoop of ice.
Process until smooth.

Calypso Colada
¾ oz. Myer's Dark Rum
¾ oz. Tia Maria
2 oz. Pina Colada Mix

Combine all ingredients in a
blender with a scoop of ice.
Process until smooth.

Calypso Daiquiri
1 ¼ oz. Myer's Dark Rum
2 oz. Sour Mix
½ oz. Cream
1 ripe Banana
1 tsp. Vanilla Extract

Combine all ingredients in a
blender with a scoop of ice.
Process until smooth.

Candy Bar
¾ oz. Frangelico
¾ oz. Dark Creme de Cacao
1 scoop Vanilla Ice Cream

Combine all ingredients in a
blender with a scoop of ice.
Process until smooth.

Candy Cane
1 oz. White Creme de Menthe
1 oz. Peppermint Schnapps
2 oz. Cream

Combine all ingredients in a
blender with a scoop of ice.
Process until smooth. Top
with a dash of Grenadine and
Green Crème de Menthe.

Candy Dandy
1 ½ oz. Captain Morgan
Parrot Bay Rum
1 oz. Brandy
1 oz. Vodka
2 tbs. Chocolate Syrup
1 scoop Vanilla Ice Cream

Combine all ingredients in a
blender. Process until smooth.

Canyon Quake
¾ oz. Baileys Irish Cream
¾ oz. Brandy
1 oz. Amaretto
2 oz. Cream

Combine all ingredients in a
blender with a scoop of ice.
Process until smooth.

Cape Colada
¾ oz. Vodka
¾ oz. Peach Schnapps
2 oz. Cranberry Juice
1 oz. Sour Mix
2 oz. Coco Lopez

Combine all ingredients in a blender with a scoop of ice. Process until smooth. Garnish with a pineapple chunk.

Cappuccino Nut
¾ oz. Baileys Irish Cream
¾ oz. Frangelico
1 ½ oz. Cold Cappuccino

Combine all ingredients in a blender with a scoop of ice. Process until smooth. Top with whipped cream.

Captain's Chocolate Covered Banana
1 ¼ oz. Captain Morgan Parrot Bay Rum
2 tbs. Chocolate Syrup
½ of a Ripe Banana
1 scoop Vanilla Ice Cream

Combine all ingredients in a blender. Process until smooth.

Captain's Colada
1 ¼ oz. Captain Morgan Spiced Rum
6 oz. Pina Colada Mix

Combine all ingredients in a blender with a scoop of ice. Process until smooth. Garnish with a pineapple stick and a cherry.

Captain's Lady
1 ¼ oz. Captain Morgan Spiced Rum
2 oz. Pineapple Juice
1 scoop Pineapple Sherbet

Combine all ingredients in a blender with a scoop of ice. Process until smooth. Garnish with a pineapple wedge and a cherry.

Captain's Peach Daiquiri
1 oz. Captain Morgan Spiced Rum
¼ oz. Peach Schnapps
4 oz. Pureed Peaches
3 oz. Sour Mix

Combine all ingredients in a blender with a scoop of ice. Process until smooth. Garnish with a fresh peach slice and a sprig of fresh mint.

Captain's Spice
1 ¼ oz. Captain Morgan Spiced Rum
2 oz. Pina Colada Mix

Combine all ingredients in a blender with a scoop of ice. Process until smooth.

Caramel Nut
1 oz. Light Creme de Cacao
1 oz. Caramel Liqueur
1 scoop Vanilla Ice Cream

Combine all ingredients in a blender. Process until smooth. Top with whipped cream and chopped nuts.

Caribbean Cruise
1 oz. Myer's Dark Rum
¾ oz. Bacardi Black Rum
¾ oz. Tia Maria
¾ oz. Coco Lopez
2 oz. Orange Juice
2 oz. Pineapple Juice

Combine all ingredients in a blender with a scoop of ice. Process until smooth. Garnish with a cherry.

Caribbean Daze
1 ¼ oz. Malibu Rum
1 ¼ oz. Raspberry Schnapps
2 oz. Pina Colada Mix

Combine all ingredients in a blender with a scoop of ice. Process until smooth.

Caribbean Dream
1 ½ oz. Light Rum
1 ½ oz. Dark Rum
1 ½ oz. Coco Lopez
2 oz. Fruit Punch
2 oz. Pineapple Juice
¼ oz. Cream

Combine all ingredients in a blender with a scoop of ice. Process until smooth.

Caribbean Grasshopper
¾ oz. Green Creme de Menthe
¾ oz. Light Creme de Cacao
2 oz. Pina Colada Mix

Combine all ingredients in a blender with a scoop of ice. Process until smooth.

Carmel Apple

1 oz. Apple Brandy
½ oz. Alize Passion Fruit Liqueur
1 oz. Cranberry Juice
2 oz. Sparkling Cider
1 tsp. Caramel Dip

Combine all ingredients in a blender with a scoop of ice. Process until smooth. Top with whipped cream a sprinkle of cinnamon.

Carmen Miranda

1 oz. Vodka
1 oz. Gold Rum
¼ oz. Lime Juice
1 small Ripe Banana

Combine all ingredients in a blender with a scoop of ice. Process until smooth.

Casablanca

½ oz. Captain Morgan Spiced Rum
½ oz. Creme de Noyeaux
¼ oz. Apricot Brandy
4 oz. Orange Juice
½ oz. Simple Syrup

Combine all ingredients in a blender with a scoop of ice. Process until smooth.

Cavanaugh Special

1 oz. Coffee Liqueur
1 oz. Light Creme de Cacao
1 oz. Amaretto
2 scoops Vanilla Ice Cream

Combine all ingredients in a blender. Process until smooth. Top with whipped cream and chocolate sprinkles.

Chambord Colada

1 ½ oz. Chambord
1 ½ oz. Light Rum
2 oz. Pineapple Juice
½ oz. Coco Lopez

Combine all ingredients in a blender with a scoop of ice. Process until smooth.

Chambord Daiquiri

¾ oz. Chambord
¾ oz. Light Rum
½ oz. Lime Juice
1 tsp. Sugar

Combine all ingredients in a blender with ½ scoop of ice. Process until smooth. Serve in a champagne glass.

Chambord Frappe

1 ½ oz. Chambord
½ oz. Light Creme de Cacao
1 scoop Vanilla Ice Cream
1 scoop Raspberry Ice Cream

Combine all ingredients in a blender. Process until smooth. Top with whipped cream.

Chambord Meltdown

1 oz. Tequila
1 oz. Triple Sec
1 oz. Sour Mix
½ oz. Lime Juice

Combine all ingredients in a blender with a scoop of ice. Process until smooth. Top with ½ oz. Chambord.

Chameleon

1 ¼ oz. Midori Melon Liqueur
1 ¼ oz. Creme de Banana
2 oz. Pina Colada Mix

Combine all ingredients in a blender with a scoop of ice. Process until smooth.

Champagne Cornucopia

1 oz. Cranberry Juice
2 scoops Rainbow Sherbet
1 oz. Vodka
¾ oz. Peach Schnapps
1 oz. Champagne

Pour cranberry juice into a hurricane glass. In a blender, combine sherbet, vodka, and peach schnapps. Process until smooth. Pour into glass. Top with Champagne.

Charlie's Angel

1 oz. Brandy
1 oz. White Creme de Menthe
1 scoop Vanilla Ice Cream

Combine all ingredients in a blender. Process until smooth.

Checkerboard

1 oz. Amaretto
½ oz. Dark Creme de Cacao
½ oz. Vodka
1 scoop Vanilla Ice Cream
¼ oz. Chocolate Syrup
1 tsp. Vanilla Extract

Combine all ingredients in a blender. Process until smooth. Top with shaved chocolate.

Cherry Daiquiri
1 ½ oz. Light Rum
½ oz. Cherry Liqueur
½ oz. Lime Juice
¼ oz. Kirsch

Combine all ingredients in a blender with a scoop of ice. Process until smooth. Garnish with a cherry.

Cherry Repair Kit
½ oz. Light Creme de Cacao
½ oz. Amaretto
½ oz. Cream
½ oz. Cherry Juice
6 Cherries

Combine all ingredients in a blender with a scoop of ice. Process until smooth. Garnish with a cherry.

Chicago Bomb
1 oz. Light Creme de Cacao
1 oz. Green Creme de Menthe
1 scoop Vanilla Ice Cream

Combine all ingredients in a blender. Process until smooth.

Chilly Irishman
1 oz. Irish Whiskey
½ oz. Baileys Irish Cream
½ oz. Kahlua
3 oz. Cold Espresso
1 scoop Vanilla Ice Cream
1 tsp. Sugar

Combine all ingredients in a blender. Process until smooth.

Chiquita
1 ½ oz. Vodka
½ oz. Creme de Banana
¼ oz. Lime Juice
1 tsp. Sugar
1 whole Ripe Banana

Combine all ingredients in a blender with a scoop of ice. Process until smooth.

Choco Colada
1 ½ oz. Light Rum
¼ oz. Kahlua
½ oz. Dark Rum
¾ oz. Coco Lopez
¾ oz. Chocolate Syrup
2 oz. Cream

Combine all ingredients in a blender with a scoop of ice. Process until smooth. Top with whipped cream.

Choc-O-Banana
1 oz. Coffee Liqueur
½ oz. Dark Creme de Cacao
1 oz. Creme de Banana
2 oz. Coco Lopez
1 oz. Cream
1 oz. Chocolate Syrup

Combine all ingredients in a blender with a scoop of ice. Process until smooth.

Choco-Banana Smash
1 ¼ oz. Baileys Irish Cream
½ oz. Licor 43
½ oz. Cream
1 scoop Vanilla Ice Cream
½ of a Ripe Banana

Combine all ingredients in a blender. Process until smooth. Top with whipped cream and chocolate sprinkles.

Chocolate Almond
1 oz. Dark Creme de Cacao
¾ oz. Amaretto
1 oz. Cream
1 scoop Vanilla Ice Cream

Combine all ingredients in a blender. Process until smooth.

Chocolate Almond Kiss
½ oz. Frangelico
½ oz. Dark Creme de Cacao
½ oz. Vodka
2 scoops Vanilla Ice Cream

Combine all ingredients in a blender. Process until smooth. Top with chocolate sprinkles.

Chocolate Banana Pina Colada
2 oz. Light Rum
2 oz. Pineapple Juice
1 oz. Coco Lopez
½ oz. Chocolate Syrup
1 whole Ripe Banana

Combine all ingredients in a blender with a scoop of ice. Process until smooth. Top with whipped cream and grated coconut.

Chocolate Black Russian
1 oz. Kahlua
1 oz. Vodka
2 scoops Chocolate Ice Cream

Combine all ingredients in a blender. Process until smooth.

Chocolate Chip Sambuca
1 ½ oz. White Sambuca
1 scoop Chocolate Chip Ice
Cream

Combine both ingredients in a
blender. Process until smooth.

Chocolate Colada
2 oz. Rum
1 oz. Chocolate Syrup
2 oz. Coco Lopez
2 oz. Cream

Combine all ingredients in a
blender with a scoop of ice.
Process until smooth.

Chocolate Covered Banana
¾ oz. Creme de Banana
½ oz. Creme de Noyeaux
½ oz. Light Creme de Cacao
2 oz. Cream
½ of a Ripe Banana

Combine all ingredients in a
blender with a scoop of ice.
Process until smooth.

Chocolate Kiss
¾ oz. Rum
¾ oz. Dark Creme de Cacao
1 scoop Vanilla Ice Cream

Combine both ingredients in a
blender. Process until smooth.

Chocolate Mint
1 oz. White Creme de Menthe
1 oz. Dark Creme de Cacao

Combine both ingredients in a
blender with a scoop of ice.
Process until smooth. Top
with whipped cream and
chocolate sprinkles.

Chocolate Mint Freeze
1 ½ oz. Dr. McGillicuddy's
Menthomint Schnapps
½ oz. Light Creme de Cacao
1 scoop Vanilla Ice Cream
¼ oz. Chocolate Syrup

Combine both ingredients in a
blender. Process until smooth.
Garnish with a chocolate chip

Chocolate Monkey
1 ½ oz. Creme de Banana
1 ½ oz. Dark Creme de Cacao
1 scoop Vanilla Ice Cream

Combine all ingredients in a
blender. Process until smooth.
Top with whipped cream and
a cherry.

Chocolate Raspberry Cream
1 ½ oz. Vodka
1 oz. Light Creme de Cacao
2 oz. Cream
2 scoops Raspberry Ice Cream

Combine all ingredients in a
blender. Process until smooth.

Chocolate Snow Bear
1 oz. Amaretto
1 oz. Light Creme de Cacao
2 scoops Vanilla Ice Cream
1 tsp. Vanilla Extract

Combine both ingredients in a
blender. Process until smooth.
Top with whipped cream and
a drizzle of chocolate syrup.

Chocolate Zam
2 oz. Absolut Citron Vodka
3 oz. Chocolate Syrup

Combine both ingredients in a
blender with a scoop of ice.
Process until smooth.

Chocolatier
1 oz. Rum
1 oz. Dark Creme de Cacao
2 scoops Chocolate Ice Cream

Combine all ingredients in a
blender. Process until smooth.
Top with whipped cream and
shaved chocolate.

Cinnamon Stick
¾ oz. Godiva Chocolate
Liqueur
¾ oz. Baileys Irish Cream
¾ oz. Kahlua
Dash of Ground Cinnamon

Combine all ingredients in a
blender with a scoop of ice.
Process until smooth.

Citron Chi Chi
1 ½ oz. Absolut Citron Vodka
1 ½ oz. Coco Lopez
¾ oz. Pineapple Juice

Combine all ingredients in a
blender with a scoop of ice.
Process until smooth.
Garnish with a cherry.

Citrus Banana Flip
1 oz. Dark Rum
1 oz. Lime Juice
1 oz. Cream
1 oz. Orange Juice
½ of a Ripe Banana

Combine all ingredients in a blender with a scoop of ice. Process until smooth. Top with a splash of club soda.

Cloud Nine
1 oz. Baileys Irish Cream
½ oz. Chambord
1 oz. Amaretto
1 scoop Vanilla Ice Cream

Combine all ingredients in a blender. Process until smooth. Top with whipped cream and a Reese's Peanut Butter Cup.

Club Paradise
1 oz. Light Rum
½ oz. Creme de Banana
½ oz. Light Creme de Cacao
1 oz. Cream
1 scoop Vanilla Ice Cream

Combine all ingredients in a blender. Process until smooth. Top with a sprinkle of ground nutmeg. Garnish with a banana slice and a cherry.

Coco Banana
1 oz. Amaretto
¾ oz. Creme de Banana
3 oz. Pina Colada Mix
½ of a Ripe Banana

Combine all ingredients in a blender with a scoop of ice. Process until smooth. Garnish with a banana slice and freshly grated coconut.

Coco Cabana
1 oz. Malibu Rum
1 oz. Creme de Banana
1 scoop Vanilla Ice Cream

Combine all ingredients in a blender. Process until smooth.

Coco Cow
1 oz. Captain Morgan Spiced Rum
1 oz. Coco Lopez
2 oz. Cream

Combine all ingredients in a blender with a scoop of ice. Process until smooth.

Coco Cranberry Smoothie
2 oz. Lime Juice
4 oz. Cranberry Juice
2 oz. Coco Lopez
1 whole Ripe Banana

Combine all ingredients in a blender with a scoop of ice. Process until smooth. Garnish with a pineapple spear and a fresh cranberry.

Coco Loco
1 ½ oz. Tequila
3 oz. Pineapple Juice
2 oz. Coco Lopez
¼ oz. Grated Coconut

Combine all ingredients in a blender with a scoop of ice. Process until smooth. Garnish with a pineapple spear.

Coco Madness
1 oz. Frangelico
1 oz. Malibu Rum
1 oz. Godiva Chocolate Liqueur
2 scoops Vanilla Ice Cream

Combine all ingredients in a blender. Process until smooth. Drizzle some chocolate syrup along the inside of a hurricane glass. Pour frozen drink into the center. Top with whipped cream.

Coco Praline
1 oz. Praline Liqueur
1 oz. Vodka
2 oz. Coco Lopez
1 ½ oz. Caramel Ice Cream Topping

Combine all ingredients in a blender with a scoop of ice. Process until smooth.

Coco Rumba
½ oz. Brandy
½ oz. Dark Creme de Cacao
½ oz. Malibu Rum
½ oz. Light Rum
1 scoop Vanilla Ice Cream

Combine all ingredients in a blender. Process until smooth. Top with a sprinkle of ground nutmeg.

Coco Toastie
1 oz. Light Rum
½ oz. Malibu Rum
2 scoops Vanilla Ice Cream

Combine all ingredients in a blender. Process until smooth. Top with whipped cream and toasted shredded coconut.

Cocoberry Colada
1 ¼ oz. Malibu Rum
1 ¼ oz. Strawberry Liqueur
2 oz. Pina Colada Mix

Combine all ingredients in a
blender with a scoop of ice.
Process until smooth.

Cocobutter
1 oz. Butterscotch Schnapps
1 ½ oz. Pina Colada Mix
1 scoop Vanilla Ice Cream

Combine all ingredients in a
blender. Process until smooth.

Coco-Mocha Alexander
¾ oz. Captain Morgan Spiced
Rum
½ oz. Coffee Liqueur
1 oz. Cold Coffee
1 oz. Coco Lopez
1 oz. Cream

Combine all ingredients in a
blender with a scoop of ice.
Process until smooth.

Coco-Mon Cream
1 oz. Malibu Rum
1 oz. Baileys Irish Cream
2 oz. Cream
1 scoop Vanilla Ice Cream
½ tsp. Ground Cinnamon

Combine all ingredients in a
blender. Process until smooth.
Top with whipped cream.

Cocomotion
1 ½ oz. Dark Rum
2 oz. Lime Juice
4 oz. Coco Lopez

Combine all ingredients in a
blender with a scoop of ice.
Process until smooth.

Coconapple
1 oz. Apple Schnapps
1 oz. Malibu Rum
1 oz. Coco Lopez
2 oz. Pineapple Juice

Combine all ingredients in a
blender with a scoop of ice.
Process until smooth.

Coconut Bellini
3 oz. Champagne
½ oz. Peach Schnapps
2 oz. Coco Lopez
½ of a Fresh Peach

Combine all ingredients in a
blender with a scoop of ice.
Process until smooth.

Coconut Colada
1 ¼ oz. Captain Morgan
Parrot Bay Rum
1 oz. Milk
5 oz. Pineapple Juice

Combine all ingredients in a
blender with a scoop of ice.
Process until smooth.
Garnish with a pineapple
spear.

Coconut Daiquiri
1 ½ oz. Rum
½ oz. Lime Juice
1 ½ oz. Coco Lopez

Combine all ingredients in a
blender with a scoop of ice.
Process until smooth.

Coconut Frappe
2 oz. Baileys Irish Cream
1 oz. Malibu Rum
2 oz. Cream

Combine all ingredients in a
blender with a scoop of ice.
Process until smooth. Top
with shredded toasted
coconut.

Coconut Telegraph
1 oz. Bacardi Light Rum
1 oz. Chivas Regal
1 oz. Coco Lopez
2 oz. Sweetened Condensed
Milk

Combine all ingredients in a
blender with a scoop of ice.
Process until smooth. Top
with shredded coconut.

Coconut Tequila
2 oz. Tequila
1 oz. Coco Lopez
1 oz. Lemon Juice
Dash of Maraschino Liqueur

Combine all ingredients in a
blender with a scoop of ice.
Process until smooth.

Coconut Toastie
1 ½ oz. Malibu Rum
2 scoops Vanilla Ice Cream

Combine both ingredients in a blender. Process until smooth. Top with whipped cream and toasted coconut flakes.

Coconutty Colada
¾ oz. Malibu Rum
¾ oz. Amaretto
1 ½ oz. Pina Colada Mix

Combine all ingredients in a blender with a scoop of ice. Process until smooth.

Coco-Orange Cream
2 ½ oz. CocoRibe Rum
2 oz. Orange Juice
1 scoop Vanilla Ice Cream

Combine all ingredients in a blender. Process until smooth.

Coffee Brandy
1 ½ oz. Brandy
1 oz. Kahlua
2 scoops Coffee Ice Cream

Combine all ingredients in a blender. Process until smooth.

Coffee Chip
1 oz. Frangelico
1 oz. Kahlua
1 oz. Amaretto di Saronno
1 oz. Baileys Irish Cream
1 oz. Vodka
1 oz. Cream

Combine all ingredients in a blender with a scoop of ice. Process until smooth.

Coffee Colada
1 oz. Coffee Liqueur
½ oz. Rum
2 oz. Pineapple Juice
1 oz. Coco Lopez

Combine all ingredients in a blender with a scoop of ice. Process until smooth.

Coffee Cooler
¾ oz. Kahlua
½ oz. Vodka
¾ oz. Cream
½ oz. Simple Syrup
3 oz. Cold Coffee
1 scoop Vanilla Ice Cream

Combine all ingredients in a blender. Process until smooth.

Coffee Overload
1 oz. Kahlua
¾ oz. Irish Whiskey
2 oz. Cold Espresso
1 scoop Vanilla Ice Cream

Combine all ingredients in a blender. Process until smooth. Top with whipped cream and a sprinkle of cocoa powder.

Colada Blues
1 oz. Bacardi Anejo Rum
1 oz. Blueberry Schnapps
1 oz. Pineapple Juice
1 oz. Coco Lopez

Combine all ingredients in a blender with a scoop of ice. Process until smooth. Garnish with fresh blueberries.

Cold Attic
2 oz. Vodka
2 oz. Red Wine
1 whole Ripe Banana
1 oz. Chocolate Syrup
3 oz. Plain Yogurt

Combine all ingredients in a blender with a scoop of ice. Process until smooth.

Cold Buttered Rum
2 oz. Rum
2 scoops Butter Pecan Ice Cream

Combine both ingredients in a blender. Process until smooth. Top with whipped cream.

Coldcocked
1 ½ oz. Southern Comfort
2 oz. Pineapple Juice
2 oz. Cola
½ oz. Coco Lopez

Combine all ingredients in a blender with a scoop of ice. Process until smooth.

Come Again
2 oz. Captain Morgan Spiced Rum
2 oz. Amaretto
2 ½ oz. Pina Colada Mix

Combine all ingredients in a blender with a scoop of ice. Process until smooth. Garnish with a pineapple chunk and a cherry.

Cookie Monster
¾ oz. Rum
¾ oz. Dark Creme de Cacao
1 scoop Vanilla Ice Cream
1 Oreo Cookie

Combine all ingredients in a blender. Process until smooth. Top with whipped cream and some crushed Oreo cookies.

Cookies & Cream
1 ½ oz. Light Creme de Cacao
2 scoops Vanilla Ice Cream
3 Oreo Cookies

Combine all ingredients in a blender. Process until smooth. Top with whipped cream and some crushed Oreo cookies.

Cookies & Crystals
1 oz. Malibu Rum
2 oz. Cream
½ oz. Caramel Syrup

Combine all ingredients in a blender with a scoop of ice. Process until smooth.

Cool Fruit Sevilla
1 oz. Light Rum
4 oz. Port Wine
1 raw Egg
1 tsp. Powdered Sugar
1 cup Fresh Strawberries

Combine all ingredients in a blender with a scoop of ice. Process until smooth. Top with a sprinkle of nutmeg. Garnish with a strawberry.

Cool Operator
1 oz. Melon Liqueur
½ oz. Lime Juice
½ oz. Vodka
½ oz. Rum
3 oz. Grapefruit Juice
2 oz. Orange Juice

Combine all ingredients in a blender with a scoop of ice. Process until smooth. Garnish with a thin melon slice.

Coral Reef
1 ¼ oz. Rum
½ oz. Lemon Juice
½ oz. Simple Syrup
¼ oz. Grenadine

Combine all ingredients in a blender with ½ scoop of ice. Process until smooth. Serve in a martini glass.

Cornish Mule
1 oz. Coffee Liqueur
1 oz. Light Rum
1 oz. Malibu Rum
1 oz. Vodka
1 oz. Grenadine
1 oz. Lime Juice
2 oz. Orange Juice
2 oz. Pineapple Juice

Combine all ingredients in a blender with a scoop of ice. Process until smooth.

Cowboy Lemonade
1 oz. Vodka
1 oz. Draft Beer
3 oz. Lemonade

Combine all ingredients in a blender with a scoop of ice. Process until smooth.

Cran Razz
1 ½ oz. White Tequila
1 oz. Black Raspberry Liqueur
3 oz. Cranberry Juice

Combine all ingredients in a blender with a scoop of ice. Process until smooth.

Cranapple Shrub
½ oz. Cranberry Cordial
½ oz. Applejack
½ oz. Peach Schnapps
1 scoop Orange Sherbet

Combine all ingredients in a blender. Process until smooth.

Cranberry Colada
1 ½ oz. Finlandia Arctic Cranberry Vodka
1 oz. Coco Lopez
2 oz. Pineapple Juice
2 oz. Cranberry Juice
½ oz. Lemon Juice

Combine all ingredients in a blender with a scoop of ice. Process until smooth. Garnish with a cherry and a pineapple chunk.

Cranberry Cooler
1 ½ oz. Bourbon
1 ½ oz. Cranberry Juice
½ oz. Lime Juice
1 tsp. Sugar

Combine all ingredients in a blender with a scoop of ice. Process until smooth.

Cranberry Margarita
1 ½ oz. White Tequila
½ oz. Triple Sec
1 ½ oz. Lime Juice
4 oz. Cranberry Juice

Combine all ingredients in a
blender with a scoop of ice.
Process until smooth. Garnish
with a fresh strawberry.

Cream Dream
2 oz. Baileys Irish Cream
2 oz. Cream

Combine both ingredients in a
blender with a scoop of ice.
Process until smooth.

Creamy Colada
1 ¼ oz. Rum
2 oz. Pina Colada Mix
1 scoop Vanilla Ice Cream

Combine all ingredients in a
blender. Process until smooth.

Creamy Creamsicle
1 ½ oz. Licor 43
1 ½ oz. Orange Juice
1 scoop Vanilla Ice Cream

Combine all ingredients in a
blender. Process until smooth.

Creamy Gin Sour
1 oz. Gin
1 oz. Lime Juice
1 oz. Lemon Juice
1 oz. Cream
½ oz. Triple Sec
1 tsp. Sugar

Combine all ingredients in a
blender with a scoop of ice.
Process until smooth. Top
with a splash of club soda.

Creme de Menthe Parfait
½ oz. Captain Morgan Spiced
Rum
¼ oz. Light Creme de Cacao
½ oz. Green Creme de
Menthe
1 oz. Coco Lopez
2 oz. Cream

Combine all ingredients in a
blender with a scoop of ice.
Process until smooth. Top
with whipped cream and a
cherry.

Cupid's Kiss
1 ¼ oz. Vodka
1 oz. Strawberry Schnapps
1 scoop Vanilla Ice Cream

Combine all ingredients in a
blender. Process until smooth.

Dark Pina Colada
1 ¼ oz. Myer's Dark Rum
4 oz. Pina Colada Mix

Combine both ingredients in a
blender with a scoop of ice.
Process until smooth. Garnish
with a pineapple stick and a
cherry.

De Fuzzy Nuts
1 oz. Peach Schnapps
1 oz. CocoRibe Rum
1 oz. Cream
2 oz. Orange Juice
2 oz. Pineapple Juice

Combine all ingredients in a
blender with a scoop of ice.
Process until smooth.

Death by Chocolate
1 oz. Baileys Irish Cream
1 oz. Godiva Chocolate
Liqueur
½ oz. Vodka
1 scoop Chocolate Ice Cream

Combine all ingredients in a
blender. Process until smooth.

De-Minted De-Light
1 ¼ oz. Smirnoff Vodka
1 oz. Triple Sec
2 ½ oz. Lime Juice
1 tsp. Sugar

Combine all ingredients in a
blender with a scoop of ice.
Process until smooth. Garnish
with a fresh sprig of mint.

Derby Daiquiri
1 ½ oz. Light Rum
1 oz. Orange Juice
¼ oz. Lime Juice
1 tsp. Sugar

Combine all ingredients in a
blender with ½ scoop of ice.
Process until smooth. Serve in
a champagne flute.

Devil's Tail
1 ½ oz. Rum
1 oz. Vodka
¼ oz. Grenadine
¼ oz. Apricot Brandy

Combine all ingredients in a
blender with a scoop of ice.
Process until smooth. Serve in
a champagne flute. Garnish
with a twist of lime.

Di Amore Dream
1 ½ oz. Amaretto
¾ oz. Light Creme de Cacao
2 oz. Orange Juice
1 scoop Vanilla Ice Cream

Combine all ingredients in a
blender. Process until smooth.
Garnish with an orange slice.

Dimpled Duchess
1 ½ oz. Amaretto di Saronno
1 scoop Strawberry Ice Cream

Combine both ingredients in a
blender. Process until smooth.
Garnish with a strawberry.

Dirty Banana
1 oz. Vodka
½ oz. 99 Bananas
1 oz. Kahlua
½ of a Ripe Banana
2 Oreo Cookies
2 oz. Cream

Combine all ingredients in a
blender with a scoop of ice.
Process until smooth. Top
with whipped cream and a
banana slice.

Dirty Nutty Banana
¾ oz. Frangelico
¾ oz. Rum
¾ oz. Dark Creme de Cacao
¾ oz. Creme de Banana
1 scoop Vanilla Ice Cream

Combine both ingredients in a
blender. Process until smooth.

DiSarita
½ oz. Amaretto di Saronno
1 oz. Cuervo Gold Tequila
3 oz. Margarita Mix

Combine both ingredients in a
blender with ½ scoop of ice.
Process until smooth. Pour
into a salt-rimmed margarita
glass. Garnish with a slice of
lime.

Dizzy Daisy
1 ¼ oz. Vodka
¾ oz. Creme de Banana
2 oz. Cream
2 oz. Fresh Strawberries

Combine all ingredients in a
blender with a scoop of ice.
Process until smooth.

Dominican Coco Loco
1 ½ oz. Light Rum
½ oz. Amaretto
½ oz. Pineapple Juice
1 oz. Coco Lopez
¼ oz. Cream
Dash of Grenadine

Combine all ingredients in a
blender with a scoop of ice.
Process until smooth.

Dream Shake
1 ½ oz. Baileys Irish Cream
¾ oz. Amaretto
4 oz. Ginger Ale
2 scoops Vanilla Ice Cream

Combine all ingredients in a
blender. Process until smooth.

Dreamy Monkey
1 oz. Vodka
½ oz. Dark Creme de Cacao
½ oz. Creme de Banana
1 oz. Cream
1 whole Ripe Banana
1 scoop Vanilla Ice Cream

Combine all ingredients in a
blender. Process until smooth.

E Pluribus Unum
¾ oz. Frangelico
¾ oz. Chambord
¾ oz. Kahlua
2 scoops Chocolate Ice Cream

Combine all ingredients in a
blender. Process until smooth.
Top with shaved white
chocolate.

Earthquake
1 ½ oz. Tequila
¼ oz. Grenadine
2 Strawberries
2 Dashes Orange Bitters

Combine all ingredients in a
blender with a scoop of ice.
Process until smooth. Garnish
with a lime twist.

Eggnog
1 ½ oz. Brandy
4 oz. Milk
1 tsp. Powdered Sugar
Dash of Bitters
1 raw Egg

Combine all ingredients in a
blender with a scoop of ice.
Process until smooth. Top
with whipped cream and a
sprinkle of nutmeg.

El Grito
1 ½ oz. Cuervo 1800 Tequila
4 oz. Fresh Strawberries
2 tsp. Sugar

Combine all ingredients in a
blender with a scoop of ice.
Process until smooth.
Garnish with a strawberry.

Electric Screwdriver
1 ½ oz. Vodka
2 oz. Cream
2 oz. Orange Juice
1 raw Egg
1 tsp. Vanilla Extract
1 tbs. Sugar

Combine all ingredients in a
blender with ½ scoop ice.
Process until smooth.

Emerald Isle Cooler
1 oz. Green Creme de Menthe
1 oz. Irish Whiskey
1 oz. Club Soda
1 scoop Vanilla Ice Cream

Combine all ingredients in a
blender. Process until smooth.

Erupting Volcano Cooler
1 ½ oz. Light Rum
2 oz. Orange Juice
2 oz. Cream
Dash of Lemon Juice
1 oz. Club Soda
2 scoops Rainbow Sherbet

Combine all ingredients in a
blender. Process until smooth.
Garnish with an orange slice.

Eskimo
2 oz. Brandy
½ oz. Maraschino Liqueur
½ oz. Orange Curacao
1 scoop Vanilla Ice Cream

Combine all ingredients in a
blender. Process until smooth.

Eve's Apple Daiquiri
1 ¼ oz. Captain Morgan
Spiced Rum
2 oz. Sour Mix
2 oz. Frozen Apple Juice

Combine all ingredients in a
blender with a scoop of ice.
Process until smooth. Garnish
with an apple wedge.

54 T-Bird
¾ oz. Grand Marnier
¾ oz. Amaretto
¾ oz. Southern Comfort
1 ½ oz. Pina Colada Mix

Combine all ingredients in a
blender with a scoop of ice.
Process until smooth.

5th Avenue
¾ oz. Godiva Chocolate
Liqueur
¾ oz. Baileys Irish Cream
¾ oz. Frangelico
1 scoop Vanilla Ice Cream

Combine all ingredients in a
blender. Process until smooth.
Top with whipped cream and
shaved dark chocolate.

Fab
1 oz. Amaretto
¾ oz. Coco Lopez
2 scoops Chocolate Ice Cream

Combine all ingredients in a
blender. Process until smooth.
Top with whipped cream and
a drizzle of chocolate syrup.

Fairy Godmother
1 oz. Amaretto
1 oz. Vodka
2 scoops Vanilla Ice Cream

Combine all ingredients in a
blender. Process until smooth.

Fan Tan
1 oz. Vodka
½ oz. Gold Rum
¾ oz. Kahlua
2 oz. Cream

Combine all ingredients in a
blender with a scoop of ice.
Process until smooth.

Fat Farmer
2 oz. Seagram's 7
2 scoops Lemon Sherbet

Combine both ingredients in a
blender. Process until smooth.

Feeler
1 ½ oz. Light Rum
½ oz. Galliano
¼ oz. Passion Fruit Syrup
¼ oz. Pineapple Juice
¼ oz. Lemon Juice

Combine all ingredients in a
blender with a scoop of ice.
Process until smooth.

Fierce Frosty
1 oz. Light Creme de Cacao
1 oz. White Creme de Menthe
1 oz. Vodka

Combine all ingredients in a blender with ½ scoop of ice. Process until smooth. Pour into a champagne flute. Float ½ oz. Kahlua on top.

Fiesta of the Bells
1 ¼ oz. Cuervo White Tequila
¾ oz. Triple Sec
1 ¼ oz. Frangelico
1 ½ oz. Sour Mix

Combine all ingredients in a blender with a scoop of ice. Process until smooth. Pour into a salt-rimmed margarita glass. Garnish with a lime wedge.

Fire Ant
1 oz. Apricot Brandy
1 oz. Cherry Brandy
1 oz. Gin
1 ½ oz. Butterscotch Schnapps
1 scoop Vanilla Ice Cream

Combine all ingredients in a blender. Process until smooth. Top with a cherry.

Flaming Gay
1 ½ oz. Vodka
1 ½ oz. Apple Brandy
2 oz. Pineapple Juice
1 oz. Coco Lopez
1 oz. Chocolate Syrup

Combine all ingredients in a blender with a scoop of ice. Process until smooth. Float ½ oz. tequila on top.

Flicker
2 oz. Light Rum
¼ oz. Lemon Juice
¼ oz. Lime Juice
¼ oz. Passion Fruit Syrup

Combine all ingredients in a blender with a scoop of ice. Process until smooth. Garnish with a cherry.

Flying Gorilla
½ oz. Creme de Banana
½ oz. Light Creme de Cacao
½ oz. Vodka
1 oz. Cream
2 scoops Vanilla Ice Cream

Combine all ingredients in a blender. Process until smooth. Garnish with a slice of fresh banana.

Forbidden Jungle
¾ oz. Kahlua
¾ oz. Baileys Irish Cream
¾ oz. Vodka
¾ oz. Creme de Banana
1 scoop Vanilla Ice Cream

Combine all ingredients in a blender. Process until smooth.

Foxy Lady
1 oz. Gin
1 oz. Triple Sec
2 scoops Vanilla Ice Cream

Combine all ingredients in a blender. Process until smooth.

Frangelico Alexander
1 oz. Frangelico
1 oz. Brandy
1 scoop Vanilla Ice Cream

Combine all ingredients in a blender. Process until smooth.

French Cream Punch
1 oz. Amaretto
1 oz. Kahlua
¼ oz. Triple Sec
1 scoop Vanilla Ice Cream

Combine all ingredients in a blender. Process until smooth.

French Dream
1 oz. Chambord
1 oz. Baileys Irish Cream
1 oz. Cream

Combine all ingredients in a blender with a ½ scoop ice. Process until smooth. Pour into a champagne flute.

Frivolous Filly
1 ½ oz. Midori Melon Liqueur
1 ½ oz. Brandy
2 slices Kiwi
1 scoop Vanilla Ice Cream

Combine all ingredients in a blender. Process until smooth.

Frog in a Blender
1 ½ oz. Tequila
½ oz. Sloe Gin
Dash of Sweet Vermouth

Shake all ingredients with crushed ice. Garnish with a cherry and a lime wedge.

Frosted Friar
1 ¼ oz. Frangelico
¾ oz. Strawberry Liqueur
1 scoop Vanilla Ice Cream

Combine all ingredients in a
blender. Process until smooth.
Top with whipped cream and
a drizzle of Frangelico.

Frosty Noggin
1 ½ oz. Rum
¾ oz. White Creme de
Menthe
3 oz. Egg Nog
1 scoop Vanilla Ice Cream

Combine all ingredients in a
blender. Process until smooth.
Top with whipped cream and
a drizzle of Green Creme de
Menthe.

Frozen Alligator
1 ¼ oz. Melon Liqueur
1 ½ oz. Pina Colada Mix
1 scoop Vanilla Ice Cream

Combine all ingredients in a
blender. Process until smooth.

Frozen Apple
1 ¼ oz. Laird's Applejack
½ oz. Lime Juice
1 tsp. Sugar
1 raw Egg

Combine all ingredients in a
blender with ½ scoop of ice.
Process until smooth.

Frozen Apple & Banana
1 ½ oz. Apple Brandy
½ oz. Creme de Banana
¼ oz. Lime Juice

Combine all ingredients in a
blender with ½ scoop of ice.
Process until smooth.

Frozen Banana Smoothie
1 ½ oz. Creme de Banana
1 oz. Mount Gay Rum
½ oz. Sour Mix
½ of a Ripe Banana

Combine all ingredients in a
blender with a scoop of ice.
Process until smooth.

Frozen Berkeley
1 ½ oz. Light Rum
½ oz. Brandy
¼ oz. Passion Fruit Juice
¼ oz. Lemon Juice

Combine all ingredients in a
blender with ½ scoop of ice.
Process until smooth. Serve in
a champagne flute.

Frozen Black Currant
1 oz. Creme de Cassis
1 oz. Pineapple Juice
¼ oz. Brandy

Combine all ingredients in a
blender with ½ scoop of ice.
Process until smooth.

Frozen Black Irish
¾ oz. Baileys Irish Cream
¾ oz. Coffee Liqueur
¾ oz. Vodka
1 scoop Chocolate Ice Cream

Combine all ingredients in a
blender. Process until smooth.

Frozen Brandy & Rum
1 ¼ oz. Brandy
1 ¼ oz. Rum
½ oz. Lemon Juice
1 tsp. Sugar
1 raw Egg

Combine all ingredients in a
blender with ½ scoop of ice.
Process until smooth.

Frozen Cappuccino
½ oz. Baileys Irish Cream
½ oz. Kahlua
½ oz. Frangelico
Splash of Cream
1 scoop Vanilla Ice Cream

Combine all ingredients in a
blender. Process until smooth.
Pour into a cinnamon sugar-
rimmed hurricane

Frozen Chicago
2 oz. Baileys Irish Cream
2 scoops Vanilla Ice Cream

Combine both ingredients in a
blender. Process until smooth.

Frozen Citron Neon
1 ½ oz. Absolut Citron Vodka
1 oz. Melon Liqueur
½ oz. Blue Curacao
½ oz. Lime Juice
1 oz. Sour Mix

Combine all ingredients in a blender with a scoop of ice. Process until smooth. Garnish with a lemon slice and a cherry.

Frozen Daiquiri
1 ½ oz. Light Rum
½ oz. Triple Sec
½ oz. Sour Mix
¼ oz. Lime Juice

Combine all ingredients in a blender with a scoop of ice. Process until smooth. Garnish with a lime wedge.

Frozen Fuzzy
1 oz. Peach Schnapps
½ oz. Triple Sec
½ oz. Lime Juice
½ oz. Grenadine
Splash of 7-Up

Combine all ingredients in a blender with a scoop of ice. Process until smooth. Garnish with a slice of lemon.

Frozen Julep
3 oz. Bourbon
1 ½ oz. Lemon Juice
1 tbs. Sugar

Combine all ingredients in a blender with a scoop of ice. Process until smooth. Garnish with a cherry and a fresh mint sprig.

Frozen Margarita
1 ½ oz. Tequila
½ oz. Triple Sec
1 oz. Sour Mix
½ oz. Lime Juice

Combine all ingredients in a blender with a scoop of ice. Process until smooth. Pour into a salt-rimmed margarita glass. Garnish with a lime wedge.

Frozen Matador
1 ½ oz. Tequila
2 oz. Pineapple Juice
¼ oz. Lime Juice

Combine all ingredients in a blender with ½ scoop of ice. Process until smooth. Garnish with a pineapple stick.

Frozen Mint Cookie
¾ oz. Kahlua
¾ oz. Peppermint Schnapps
1 Oreo Cookie
1 scoop Vanilla Ice Cream

Combine all ingredients in a blender. Process until smooth.

Frozen Mint Daiquiri
2 oz. Light Rum
¼ oz. Lime Juice
1 tsp. Sugar
6 fresh Mint Leaves

Combine all ingredients in a blender with ½ scoop of ice. Process until smooth.

Frozen Mudslide
½ oz. Kahlua
½ oz. Baileys Irish Cream
¾ oz. Vodka
1 scoop Vanilla Ice Cream

Combine all ingredients in a blender with ½ scoop of ice. Process until smooth. Top with whipped cream and a cherry.

Frozen Nutty Italian
¾ oz. Frangelico
¾ oz. Amaretto
1 scoop Vanilla Ice Cream

Combine all ingredients in a blender. Process until smooth.

Frozen Orange Bomber
1 ½ oz. Rum
3 oz. Orange Juice
2 oz. 7-Up

Combine all ingredients in a blender with a scoop of ice. Process until smooth.

Frozen Orange Delight
1 ½ oz. Captain Morgan Spiced Rum
3 oz. Orange Juice
1 tbs. Sugar

Combine all ingredients in a blender with ½ scoop of ice. Process until smooth. Garnish with a fresh strawberry.

Frozen Passion Fruit
1 ½ oz. Light Rum
½ oz. Passion Fruit Syrup
¼ oz. Lime Juice
¼ oz. Orange Juice
Dash of Lemon Juice

Combine all ingredients in a blender with ½ scoop of ice. Process until smooth.

Frozen Pineapple Daiquiri
1 ½ oz. Light Rum
¼ oz. Lime Juice
1 tsp. Sugar
2 Pineapple Slices

Combine all ingredients in a blender with a scoop of ice. Process until smooth.

Frozen Purple Balls
1 ½ oz. Watermelon Schnapps
½ oz. Blue Curacao

Combine both ingredients in a blender with a scoop of ice. Process until smooth. Serve in a shooter glass.

Frozen Raspberry Sherbet
1 oz. Chambord
1 oz. Razzmatazz
½ oz. Vodka
3 oz. Cream

Combine all ingredients in a blender with a scoop of ice. Process until smooth.

Frozen Rum Honey
2 oz. Bacardi 151 Rum
½ oz. Honey
¼ oz. Lemon Juice

Combine all ingredients in a blender with ½ scoop of ice. Process until smooth.

Frozen Shaker
1 ½ oz. White Sambuca
1 oz. Rye Whiskey
2 oz. Cream
2 oz. Fresh Strawberries
1 scoop Vanilla Ice Cream

Combine all ingredients in a blender. Process until smooth.

Frozen Steps
1 oz. Vodka
½ oz. Dark Creme de Cacao
1 scoop Vanilla Ice Cream

Combine all ingredients in a blender. Process until smooth.

Frozen Strawberry Delicious
1 ½ oz. Rum
½ oz. Lime Juice
3 oz. Pineapple Juice
3 oz. Fresh Strawberries
1 tsp. Sugar

Combine all ingredients in a blender with a scoop of ice. Process until smooth.

Fruits & Nuts
1 oz. Creme de Noyeaux
¾ oz. Creme de Cassis
1 ½ oz. Sour Mix

Combine all ingredients in a blender with a scoop of ice. Process until smooth.

Fruity Loopy
3 oz. Vodka
3 oz. Frozen Berries
3 oz. Frozen Concentrated Orange Juice

Combine all ingredients in a blender. Process until smooth.

Fruity Smash
1 oz. Cherry Brandy
1 oz. Creme de Banana
1 scoop Vanilla Ice Cream

Combine all ingredients in a blender. Process until smooth. Garnish with a cherry.

Funky Monkey
¾ oz. Rum
¾ oz. Kahlua
¾ oz. Creme de Banana
1 oz. Pina Colada Mix
1 scoop Vanilla Ice Cream

Combine all ingredients in a blender. Process until smooth.

Funky Shake
2 oz. Vodka
1 oz. Cream
1 scoop Vanilla Ice Cream

Combine all ingredients in a blender. Process until smooth.

Fuzzy Charlie
¾ oz. Captain Morgan Spiced Rum
¾ oz. Peach Schnapps
2 oz. Pina Colada Mix
4 oz. Orange Juice

Combine all ingredients in a blender with a scoop of ice. Process until smooth.

Gaelic Coffee
¾ oz. Irish Whiskey
¾ oz. Baileys Irish Cream
1 ½ oz. Dark Creme de Cacao
2 oz. Cream
1 tsp. Instant Coffee Powder

Combine all ingredients in a blender with a ½ scoop of ice. Process until smooth. Top with whipped cream and a drizzle of Green Crème de Menthe.

Galliano Daiquiri
¾ oz. Galliano
¾ oz. Light Rum
1 tsp. Sugar
1 oz. Fresh Lime Juice

Combine all ingredients in a blender with a ½ scoop of ice. Process until smooth. Garnish with a slice of lime.

Gang Green Colada
1 ½ oz. Rum
1 oz. Midori Melon Liqueur
3 oz. Pina Colada Mix

Combine all ingredients in a blender with a scoop of ice. Process until smooth.

Gauguin
2 oz. Light Rum
¼ oz. Passion Fruit Syrup
¼ oz. Lemon Juice
¼ oz. Lime Juice

Combine all ingredients in a blender with a scoop of ice. Process until smooth. Garnish with a cherry.

Georgia Peach Punch
1 oz. Smirnoff Vodka
½ oz. Peach Schnapps
3 oz. Peach Puree
1 oz. Peach Monin

Combine all ingredients in a blender with a ½ scoop of ice. Process until smooth. Top with a squeeze of fresh lemon juice.

Georgio
1 oz. Kahlua
1 oz. Baileys Irish Cream
1 oz. Cream
½ of a Ripe Banana

Combine all ingredients in a blender with a scoop of ice. Process until smooth. Top with whipped cream and a sprinkle of cocoa powder.

Gigantic White
1 oz. Baileys Irish Cream
1 oz. Sloe Gin
2 oz. Cream
1 oz. Pineapple Juice
½ oz. Coco Lopez

Combine all ingredients in a blender with a scoop of ice. Process until smooth. Top with whipped cream.

Ginger Colada
1 oz. Canton Delicate Ginger Liqueur
½ oz. Rum
1 ½ oz. Coco Lopez

Combine all ingredients in a blender with a scoop of ice. Process until smooth.

Gingersnap
¾ oz. Captain Morgan Spiced Rum
½ oz. Ginger Brandy
4 oz. Prepared Egg Nog
1 Ginger Snap

Combine all ingredients in a blender with ½ scoop of ice. Process until smooth. Garnish with a ginger snap.

Godiva Almond Joy
1 ¾ oz. Godiva Chocolate Liqueur
½ oz. Frangelico
1 oz. Coco Lopez

Combine all ingredients in a blender with a scoop of ice. Process until smooth.

Godiva Chocolate Covered Banana
2 oz. Godiva Chocolate Liqueur
½ oz. Myer's Dark Rum
½ of a Ripe Banana
1 scoop Vanilla Ice Cream

Combine all ingredients in a blender. Process until smooth. Garnish with a slice of banana.

Godiva Whisper
¾ oz. Godiva Chocolate Liqueur
½ oz. Martell Cognac
2 scoops Vanilla Ice Cream

Combine all ingredients in a blender. Process until smooth.

Golden Frog
1 oz. Vodka
½ oz. Galliano
¼ oz. Strega
¼ oz. Lemon Juice

Combine all ingredients in a blender with ½ scoop of ice. Process until smooth.

Golden Sunset
1 ½ oz. Cuervo Gold Tequila
3 oz. 7-Up
3 oz. Fresh Pineapple

Combine all ingredients in a blender with a scoop of ice. Process until smooth. Garnish with a pineapple chunk.

Golden Torpedo
1 oz. Galliano
1 oz. Amaretto
1 scoop Vanilla Ice Cream

Combine all ingredients in a blender. Process until smooth.

Goombay Smash
¾ oz. Bacardi 151 Rum
¾ oz. CocoRibe Rum
1 oz. Coco Lopez
3 oz. Pineapple Juice

Combine all ingredients in a blender with a scoop of ice. Process until smooth. Garnish with a pineapple slice and a cherry.

Grape Freeze Pop
1 ½ oz. Blue Curacao
1 oz. Vodka

Combine both ingredients in a blender with a scoop of ice. Process until smooth. Top with whipped cream and a cherry.

Grapefruit Frozen Daiquiri
1 ½ oz. Grapefruit Liqueur
1 ½ oz. Sour Mix

Combine both ingredients in a blender with a scoop of ice. Process until smooth. Garnish with a cherry.

Great White Shark
¾ oz. Grand Marnier
¾ oz. Kahlua
¾ oz. Brandy
2 scoops Vanilla Ice Cream

Combine all ingredients in a blender. Process until smooth.

Green Dragon
1 ½ oz. Midori Melon Liqueur
3 oz. Coco Lopez
6 oz. Fresh Honeydew Melon

Combine all ingredients in a blender with a scoop of ice. Process until smooth.

Guinness Shake
8 oz. Guinness Stout
2 oz. Dark Creme de Cacao
½ oz. Kahlua
2 scoops Coffee Ice Cream

Combine all ingredients in a blender. Process until smooth. Pour into a pint glass.

Gulf Stream
1 oz. Blue Curacao
½ oz. Rum
½ oz. Brandy
3 oz. Champagne
3 oz. Lemonade
1 oz. Lime Juice

Combine all ingredients in a blender with a scoop of ice. Process until smooth. Pour into a champagne flute.

Haagen-Dazs Humdinger
2 oz. Haagen-Dazs Cream Liqueur
1 scoop Haagen-Dazs Rum Raisin Ice Cream

Combine both ingredients in a blender. Process until smooth.

Haagen-Dazs Nog
2 oz. Haagen-Dazs Cream Liqueur
½ oz. Rum
1 oz. Cream
1 raw Egg

Combine all ingredients in a blender with a scoop of ice. Process until smooth. Top with a sprinkle of nutmeg.

Haagen-Dazs Smith & Kerns
1 ½ oz. Haagen-Dazs Cream Liqueur
1 ½ oz. Kahlua
1 oz. Cola
1 oz. Cream

Combine all ingredients in a blender with a scoop of ice. Process until smooth. Top with whipped cream and a sprinkle of nutmeg.

Havana Banana
1 ¼ oz. Cuervo Gold Tequila
¾ oz. Creme de Banana
Juice of ½ Lemon
½ of a Ripe Banana

Combine all ingredients in a
blender with a scoop of ice.
Process until smooth. Garnish
with an orange slice and a
cherry.

Hawaii 5-0
1 ¼ oz. Captain Morgan
Spiced Rum
½ oz. Strawberry Schnapps
1 ½ oz. Pina Colada Mix
1 scoop Vanilla Ice Cream

Combine all ingredients in a
blender. Process until smooth.

Hawaiian Coffee
1 oz. Rum
2 oz. Pineapple Juice
4 oz. Cold Coffee
1 scoop Vanilla Ice Cream

Combine all ingredients in a
blender. Process until smooth.

Hawaiian Eye
1 oz. Kahlua
1 oz. Vodka
½ oz. Bourbon
1 oz. Cream
2 oz. Pineapple Juice
1 Egg White

Combine all ingredients in a
blender with a scoop of ice.
Process until smooth. Garnish

Hawaiian Punch
1 ½ oz. Southern Comfort
3 oz. Cream Soda
2 scoops Rainbow Sherbet

Combine all ingredients in a
blender. Process until smooth.

Heat Wave
1 ½ oz. Gold Rum
4 oz. Orange Juice

Combine both ingredients in a
blender with a scoop of ice.
Process until smooth.

Heavenly Ginger
1 oz. Canton Delicate Ginger
Liqueur
1 oz. Devonshire Cream
Liqueur

Combine both ingredients in a
blender with a scoop of ice.
Process until smooth.

High Tide
1 oz. Gin
1 oz. Coco Lopez
3 oz. Fresh Strawberries

Combine all ingredients in a
blender with ½ scoop of ice.
Process until smooth.
Garnish with a fresh mint
sprig.

Holly Berry
3 oz. Strawberry Liqueur
1 oz. Rum
1 oz. Myer's Rum Cream
Liqueur Dash of Grenadine
Dash of Sour Mix

Combine all ingredients in a
blender with a scoop of ice.
Process until smooth.

Horny Bull
1 ½ oz. Tequila
3 oz. Orange Juice
1 oz. Lemonade
½ oz. Grenadine

Combine all ingredients in a
blender with a scoop of ice.
Process until smooth. Garnish
with an orange wedge and a
cherry.

Horny Leprechaun
1 oz. Melon Liqueur
1 oz. Peach Schnapps
 1 oz. Vodka
2 oz. Orange Juice

Combine all ingredients in a
blender with a scoop of ice.
Process until smooth.

Hugs & Kisses
¾ oz. Frangelico
¾ oz. Godiva Chocolate
Liqueur
3 oz. Cream
1 scoop Vanilla Ice Cream
2 Hershey's Hugs (with
almonds)

Combine all ingredients in a
blender. Process until smooth.
Top with whipped cream and
a Hershey's Hug.

Hula Hula
1 ¼ oz. Melon Liqueur
1 ¼ oz. Strawberry Liqueur
2 oz. Pina Colada Mix

Combine all ingredients in a
blender with a scoop of ice.
Process until smooth.

Hummer
1 oz. Kahlua
1 oz. Light Rum
1 scoop Vanilla Ice Cream

Combine all ingredients in a blender. Process until smooth.

Hurricane
¾ oz. Captain Morgan Spiced Rum
¾ oz. Myer's Dark Rum
¾ oz. Orange Juice
1 ½ oz. Pina Colada Mix

Combine all ingredients in a blender with a scoop of ice. Process until smooth. Top with a splash of grenadine.

Hurricane Dujo
1 oz. Absolut Citron Vodka
1 oz. Bacardi Limon Rum
2 oz. Orange Soda
½ oz. Lemon Juice
1 tsp. Sugar

Combine all ingredients in a blender with a scoop of ice. Process until smooth.

Ice Cream Flip
¾ oz. Triple Sec
½ oz. Maraschino Liqueur
1 raw Egg
1 scoop Vanilla Ice Cream

Combine all ingredients in a blender. Process until smooth. Top with a sprinkle of nutmeg.

Ice Cream Sandwich
1 ½ oz. Light Creme de Cacao
1 oz. Cream
1 scoop Vanilla Ice Cream
4 Oreo Cookies

Combine all ingredients in a blender. Process until smooth. Garnish with an Oreo cookie.

Ice Cream Surprise
¾ oz. Kahlua
¾ oz. Peppermint Schnapps
¾ oz. Baileys Irish Cream
¾ oz. Butterscotch Schnapps
1 scoop Vanilla Ice Cream

Combine all ingredients in a blender. Process until smooth.

Iceball
1 ½ oz. Gin
¾ oz. White Creme de Menthe
¾ oz. White Sambuca
¼ oz. Cream

Combine all ingredients in a blender with ½ scoop of ice. Process until smooth.

Iced Brandy
1 ½ oz. Brandy
½ oz. Light Creme de Cacao
2 scoops French Vanilla Ice Cream
2 oz. Shaved Chocolate

Combine all ingredients in a blender. Process until smooth. Pour into a brandy snifter. Top with additional shaved chocolate.

Iced Coffee a L 'Orange
2 oz. Triple Sec
1 tsp. Instant Coffee Powder
1 scoop Vanilla Ice Cream

Combine all ingredients in a blender. Process until smooth. Garnish with an orange slice.

Icy Chiller
1 ½ oz. Cold Wave Liqueur
1 oz. Kahlua
½ oz. Light Creme de Cacao

Combine all ingredients in a blender with a scoop of ice. Process until smooth. Garnish with a cherry.

Icy Rummed Cacao
1 oz. Dark Rum
1 oz. Dark Creme de Cacao
1 scoop Vanilla Ice Cream

Combine all ingredients in a blender. Process until smooth. Top with shaved chocolate.

Impeachment
2 oz. Malibu Rum
1 oz. Peach Schnapps
3 oz. Cream
½ of a Ripe Peach

Combine all ingredients in a blender with a scoop of ice. Process until smooth. Garnish with a fresh peach slice.

Incredible Toasted Cappuccino
¾ oz. Kahlua
¾ oz. Amaretto
¾ oz. Frangelico
1 oz. Cold Cappuccino

Combine all ingredients in a blender with a scoop of ice. Process until smooth.

Irish Cappuccino
1 ½ oz. Irish Whiskey
4 oz. Cold Cappuccino

Combine both ingredients in a blender with a scoop of ice. Process until smooth.

Irish Coconut
¾ oz. Malibu Rum
¾ oz. Baileys Irish Cream
1 ½ oz. Pina Colada Mix

Combine all ingredients in a blender with a scoop of ice. Process until smooth.

Irish Coffee Freeze
¾ oz. Jameson Irish Whiskey
¾ oz. Kahlua
¾ oz. Light Creme de Cacao
½ oz. Cold Coffee
1 scoop Vanilla Ice Cream

Combine all ingredients in a blender with ½ scoop of ice. Process until smooth.

Irish Dream
½ oz. Frangelico
½ oz. Baileys Irish Cream
¾ oz. Dark Creme de Cacao
1 scoop Vanilla Ice Cream

Combine all ingredients in a blender. Process until smooth. Top with whipped cream and chocolate sprinkles.

Islander
1 ¼ oz. Amaretto
1 ¼ oz. Peach Schnapps
1 scoop Vanilla Ice Cream

Combine all ingredients in a blender. Process until smooth.

Isle of Coconut
1 ½ oz. Light Rum
¼ oz. Coco Lopez
¼ oz. Lime Juice
Dash of Lemon Juice
Dash of Orange Juice
1 tsp. Sugar

Combine all ingredients in a blender with a ½ scoop of ice. Process until smooth. Garnish with a pineapple chunk.

Italian Bear
1 oz. Kahlua
1 oz. Vodka
2 scoops Vanilla Ice Cream

Combine all ingredients in a blender. Process until smooth.

Italian Blizzard
1 ½ oz. Amaretto di Saronno
¼ oz. Creme de Banana
½ of a Ripe Banana
1 scoop Vanilla Ice Cream

Combine all ingredients in a blender. Process until smooth. Garnish with a slice of banana.

Italian Colada
1 ½ oz. Amaretto di Saronno
1 oz. Light Rum
3 oz. Pina Colada Mix

Combine all ingredients in a blender with a scoop of ice. Process until smooth.

Italian Dream
1 ½ oz. Baileys Irish Cream
½ oz. Amaretto
2 oz. Cream

Combine all ingredients in a blender with a scoop of ice. Process until smooth.

Italian Ice
¾ oz. Captain Morgan Spiced Rum
¾ oz. Triple Sec
¾ oz. Lime Juice
2 oz. Pina Colada Mix

Combine all ingredients in a blender with a scoop of ice. Process until smooth.

Jack Frost
1 ½ oz. Dark Creme de Cacao
1 ½ oz. Canadian Whisky
2 scoops Vanilla Ice Cream

Combine all ingredients in a blender. Process until smooth. Top with whipped cream and a sprinkle of ground nutmeg.

Jack's Jam
½ oz. Peach Schnapps
½ oz. Apple Schnapps
½ oz. Strawberry Liqueur
¼ oz. Creme de Banana
2 oz. Sour Mix
1 oz. Orange Juice

Combine all ingredients in a blender with a scoop of ice. Process until smooth. Garnish with a fresh strawberry.

Jamaican Banana
½ oz. Light Rum
½ oz. Light Creme de Cacao
1 oz. Cream
1 whole Ripe Banana
2 scoops Vanilla Ice Cream

Combine all ingredients in a blender. Process until smooth. Garnish with a banana slice, a strawberry and a cherry.

Jamaican Blues
1 ¼ oz. Light Rum
½ oz. Blue Curacao
1 ¼ oz. Pineapple Juice
1 oz. Coco Lopez

Combine all ingredients in a blender with a scoop of ice. Process until smooth.

Jamaican Me Crazy
½ oz. Myer's Dark Rum
½ oz. Captain Morgan Spiced Rum
¼ oz. Blue Curacao
2 oz. Coco Lopez
1 oz. Orange Juice
1 oz. Sour Mix

Combine all ingredients in a blender with a scoop of ice. Process until smooth. Garnish with a cherry.

Jamaican Punch
¾ oz. Myer's Dark Rum
¾ oz. Orange Juice
1 ½ oz. Pina Colada Mix
Dash of Grenadine

Combine all ingredients in a blender with a scoop of ice. Process until smooth.

Jamaican Shake
2 oz. Bourbon
1 ½ oz. Dark Rum
1 ½ oz. Cream

Combine all ingredients in a blender with ½ scoop of ice. Process until smooth.

Jasper's Freeze
1 ½ oz. Vodka
1 oz. Orange Juice
1 scoop Orange Sherbet

Combine all ingredients in a blender with a scoop of ice. Process until smooth. Top with whipped cream and a cherry.

Jasper's Nog
¾ oz. Egg Nog Liqueur
¾ oz. Light Creme de Cacao
1 oz. Cream
1 scoop Egg Nog Ice Cream

Combine all ingredients in a blender with a scoop of ice. Process until smooth. Top with whipped cream and a cherry.

Jewels
2 oz. Vodka
2 oz. Orange Juice
3 oz. Fresca
1 whole Ripe Banana

Combine all ingredients in a blender with a scoop of ice. Process until smooth.

Jump Up & Kiss Me
2 oz. Galliano
2 oz. Rum
½ oz. Apricot Brandy
1 oz. Pineapple Juice
2 Egg Whites

Combine all ingredients in a blender with a scoop of ice. Process until smooth.

Junior Mint
3 oz. Peppermint Schnapps
2 scoops Chocolate Sorbet

Combine both ingredients in a blender. Process until smooth.

Just Peachy
1 ¼ oz. Peach Brandy
½ oz. Apple Schnapps
1 oz. Cream
1 scoop Vanilla Ice Cream

Combine all ingredients in a blender with a scoop of ice. Process until smooth.

Kahlua Banana
1 ¼ oz. Kahlua
½ of a Ripe Banana
2 oz. Cream
¾ oz. Creme de Banana
1 scoop Vanilla Ice Cream

Combine all ingredients in a blender. Process until smooth. Top with whipped cream.

Kahlua Cabana
¾ oz. Kahlua
¾ oz. Rum
¾ oz. Creme de Banana
1 ½ oz. Pina Colada Mix

Combine all ingredients in a blender with a scoop of ice. Process until smooth.

Kahlua Colada
1 ½ oz. Kahlua
1 oz. Rum
½ oz. Cream
1 oz. Coco Lopez
2 oz. Pineapple Juice
½ oz. Lime Juice

Combine all ingredients in a blender with a scoop of ice. Process until smooth.

Kahlua Frost
1 ½ oz. Kahlua
1 ½ oz. Coco Lopez
2 scoops Vanilla Ice Cream

Combine all ingredients in a blender. Process until smooth.

Kahlua Hammer
1 oz. Kahlua
1 oz. Rum
2 scoops Vanilla Ice Cream

Combine all ingredients in a blender with ½ scoop of ice. Process until smooth.

Kappa Colada
1 oz. Brandy
1 oz. Coco Lopez
2 oz. Pineapple Juice

Combine all ingredients in a blender with ½ scoop of ice. Process until smooth.

Karate Chop
¾ oz. Vodka
¾ oz. Light Rum
¾ oz. Triple Sec
2 oz. Pineapple Juice
2 oz. Orange Juice
2 oz. Cherry Wine
2 oz. Sake
Dash of Coconut Extract

Combine all ingredients in a blender with a scoop of ice. Process until smooth.

Key Lime Cooler
1 ½ oz. Light Rum
1 oz. Lime Juice
1 oz. Cream
1 oz. Simple Syrup
1 scoop Vanilla Ice Cream

Combine all ingredients in a blender. Process until smooth. Top with whipped cream. Garnish with a lime wheel.

Key West Song
1 ¼ oz. Captain Morgan Spiced Rum
1 oz. Coco Lopez
2 oz. Orange Juice

Combine all ingredients in a blender with a scoop of ice. Process until smooth.

Keyahlua
1 oz. Kahlua
1 oz. Mount Gay Rum
1 scoop Vanilla Ice Cream

Combine all ingredients in a blender. Process until smooth.

Kiwi Dream
1 ½ oz. Creme de Banana
2 oz. Midori Melon Liqueur
1 ½ oz. Stolichnaya Vodka
3 oz. Pineapple Juice
1 peeled & sliced Kiwi fruit

Combine all ingredients in a blender with a scoop of ice. Process until smooth. Garnish with a slice of kiwi.

Knock Out
½ oz. Vodka
1 oz. Kahlua
1 oz. Baileys Irish Cream
1 oz. White Creme de Menthe
2 oz. Cream

Combine all ingredients in a blender with a scoop of ice. Process until smooth.

Knock You on Your Butt
1 oz. Bourbon
1 oz. Light Rum
1 oz. Cinnamon Schnapps
2 scoops Vanilla Ice Cream

Combine all ingredients in a blender. Process until smooth.

Koala Bear
1 oz. Creme de Banana
1 oz. Dark Creme de Cacao
2 scoops Vanilla Ice Cream

Combine all ingredients in a blender. Process until smooth. Top with whipped cream and a sprinkle of ground nutmeg.

Koala Kolada
¾ oz. Melon Liqueur
¾ oz. Peach Schnapps
2 oz. Crushed Pineapple
1 oz. Pineapple Juice
1 ½ oz. Coco Lopez
1 peeled & sliced Kiwi fruit

Combine all ingredients in a blender with a scoop of ice. Process until smooth.

Kokomo Joe
1 ½ oz. Rum
½ oz. Creme de Banana
½ oz. Orange Juice
2 oz. Pina Colada Mix
1 whole Ripe Banana

Combine all ingredients in a blender with a scoop of ice. Process until smooth.

Leapin' Leprechaun
¾ oz. Green Creme de Menthe
¾ oz. Light Creme de Cacao
¾ oz. Creme de Banana
1 scoop Vanilla Ice Cream

Combine all ingredients in a blender. Process until smooth.

Lebanese Snow
1 ½ oz. Strawberry Liqueur
1 oz. Creme de Banana
1 oz. Cream

Combine all ingredients in a blender with a scoop of ice. Process until smooth. Garnish with a fresh strawberry.

Lemon Delight
1 ½ oz. Malibu Rum
1 oz. Sour Mix
2 scoops Lemon Sherbet

Combine all ingredients in a blender with a scoop of ice. Process until smooth. Garnish with a lemon wedge and a cherry.

Lemonade Slush
2 oz. Vodka
1 oz. Triple Sec
1 Sliced Lemon
1 tbs. Sugar

Combine all ingredients in a blender with a scoop of ice. Process until smooth.

Lychee Nut Cocktail
1 oz. Myer's Dark Rum
¼ oz. Cherry Brandy
1 oz. Sour Mix
1 tsp. Sugar
3 Lychee Nuts

Combine all ingredients in a blender with a scoop of ice. Process until smooth. Garnish with a lime wheel and a cherry.

Licorice Mist
1 ¼ oz. White Sambuca
½ oz. Malibu Rum
2 oz. Cream

Combine all ingredients in a blender with a scoop of ice. Process until smooth. Garnish with a black licorice stick.

Lighthouse Laddie
1 oz. Light Rum
1 oz. Butterscotch Schnapps
1 oz. Dark Creme de Cacao
1 oz. Coco Lopez
2 oz. Cream

Combine all ingredients in a blender with a scoop of ice. Process until smooth.

Lili Marlene
1 oz. White Tequila
½ oz. Triple Sec
1 oz. Sour Mix
1 whole Ripe Peach
1 tsp. Sugar

Combine all ingredients in a blender with a scoop of ice. Process until smooth. Garnish with a peach slice.

Lime Daiquiri
1 ¼ oz. Rum
1 ¼ oz. Lime Juice
1 tbs. Sugar

Combine all ingredients in a blender with a scoop of ice. Process until smooth. Garnish with a lime wheel.

Lime Sour Smash
1 ½ oz. Licor 43
4 oz. Limeade

Combine both ingredients in a blender with a scoop of ice. Process until smooth. Garnish with a slice of lime.

Liquid Sex
¾ oz. Amaretto
¾ oz. Baileys Irish Cream
¾ oz. Kahlua
2 oz. Cream

Combine all ingredients in a blender with a scoop of ice. Process until smooth.

Liquid Temptation
1 ½ oz. Light Rum
½ oz. Creme de banana
4 oz. Fresh Strawberries
1 oz. Sour Mix

Combine all ingredients in a blender with a scoop of ice. Process until smooth. Garnish with a fresh banana slice.

London Freeze
2 oz. Gin
1 scoop Vanilla Ice Cream

Combine both ingredients in a blender. Process until smooth. Fill with 2 oz. club soda.

Lonely Night
1 ¼ oz. Baileys Irish Cream
1 ¼ oz. Frangelico
¼ oz. Kahlua
1 scoop Vanilla Ice Cream

Combine all ingredients in a blender. Process until smooth. Top with whipped cream and chocolate shavings.

Loom Dog
1 ½ oz. Light Rum
1 ½ oz. Orange Juice
1 ½ oz. Pineapple Juice

Combine all ingredients in a blender with a scoop of ice. Process until smooth.

Loose Moose
1 oz. Frangelico
1 oz. Light Creme de Cacao
1 oz. Strawberry Schnapps
2 oz. Cream

Combine all ingredients in a blender with a scoop of ice. Process until smooth.

Love Birds
1 ½ oz. Vodka
2 oz. Sour Mix
½ oz. Grenadine
Dash of Dark Rum

Combine all ingredients in a blender with ½ scoop of ice. Process until smooth. Garnish with a cherry.

Mac
1 ½ oz. Vodka
2 oz. White Wine
2 oz. Peach Nectar
2 oz. Apple Juice
1 tbs. Honey

Combine all ingredients in a blender with a scoop of ice. Process until smooth.

Madonna
2 oz. Tequila
1 oz. Triple Sec
¼ oz. Blue Curacao
2 oz. Sour Mix
1 whole Ripe Banana

Combine all ingredients in a blender with a scoop of ice. Process until smooth. Garnish with a lime wedge.

Madras
¾ oz. Captain Morgan Spiced
Rum
½ oz. Triple Sec
2 oz. Pineapple Juice
2 oz. Cranberry Juice
1 oz. Coco Lopez

Combine all ingredients in a
blender with a scoop of ice.
Process until smooth. Garnish
with a fresh mint leaf.

Magee Mixer
1 oz. Apple Schnapps
1 oz. Light Rum
1 oz. Vodka
1 ½ oz. Cranberry Juice
1 ½ oz. Lemonade

Combine all ingredients in a
blender with a scoop of ice.
Process until smooth.

Malibu Cool
1 ½ oz. Malibu Rum
2 oz. Pineapple Juice
1 tsp. Sugar

Combine all ingredients in a
blender with a scoop of ice.
Process until smooth. Top
with a dash of bitters.

Malibu Daiquiri
1 ½ oz. Malibu Rum
½ oz. Lime Juice
1 oz. Sour Mix

Combine all ingredients in a
blender with a scoop of ice.
Process until smooth. Garnish
with a slice of lime.

Malibu Dream
1 ½ oz. Malibu Rum
1 oz. Pina Colada Mix
1 oz. Orange Juice
1 oz. Pineapple Juice
½ oz. Grenadine

Combine all ingredients in a
blender with a scoop of ice.
Process until smooth.

Malibu Orange Colada
1 ½ oz. Malibu Rum
½ oz. Triple Sec
2 oz. Pineapple Juice
1 oz. Coco Lopez

Combine all ingredients in a
blender with a scoop of ice.
Process until smooth.

Malibu Smooth Groove
1 ½ oz. Malibu Rum
1 ½ oz. Melon Liqueur
1 ½ oz. Baileys Irish Cream
1 scoop Vanilla Ice Cream

Combine all ingredients in a
blender with a scoop of ice.
Process until smooth.

Malted Mudslide
1 oz. Vodka
1 oz. Baileys Irish Cream
1 oz. Kahlua
1 scoop Vanilla Ice Cream
5 Whoppers Candies
1 oz. Cream

Combine all ingredients in a
blender. Process until smooth.
Top with whipped cream and
crushed Whoppers candies.

Mango Colada
2 oz. Bacardi Light Rum
1 oz. Coco Lopez
½ of a Fresh Mango, peeled
2 tsp. Sugar

Combine all ingredients in a
blender with a scoop of ice.
Process until smooth. Garnish
with an orange slice and a
cherry.

Mango Daiquiri
1 oz. Myer's Dark Rum
¼ oz. Orange Curacao
3 oz. Mango
1 ½ oz. Sour Mix

Combine all ingredients in a
blender with a scoop of ice.
Process until smooth. Garnish
with an orange slice and a
cherry.

Mango Loco
1 ½ oz. Captain Morgan
Parrot Bay Rum
1 oz. Nassau Royale Liqueur
1 ½ oz. Mango Puree
1 ½ oz. Grapefruit Juice
Dash of Lime Juice

Combine all ingredients in a
blender with a scoop of ice.
Process until smooth. Garnish
with a mango chunk and a
lime wheel.

Mango Martini
1 ½ oz. Vodka
¾ oz. Triple Sec
¼ oz. Lime Juice
1 ½ oz. Mango Juice

Combine all ingredients in a
blender with a scoop of ice.
Process until smooth. Pour
into a large martini glass.

Maraschino Cherry
1 oz. Rum
½ oz. Amaretto
½ oz. Peach Schnapps
1 oz. Cranberry Juice
1 oz. Pineapple Juice
Dash of Grenadine

Combine all ingredients in a
blender with a scoop of ice.
Process until smooth. Top
with whipped cream and a
cherry.

Maui Breeze
½ oz. Amaretto
½ oz. Triple Sec
½ oz. Brandy
1 oz. Sour Mix
2 oz. Orange Juice
2 oz. Guava Juice

Combine all ingredients in a
blender with a scoop of ice.
Process until smooth. Garnish

McMonkey's Special
1 oz. 99 Bananas
1 oz. Light Creme de Cacao
½ oz. Baileys Irish Cream
¼ oz. Chocolate Syrup
1 scoop Vanilla Ice Cream
½ of a Ripe Banana

Combine all ingredients in a
blender with ½ scoop of ice.
Process until smooth. Top
with whipped cream and a
banana slice.

Medias de Seda
1 oz. Cuervo Gold Tequila
1 oz. Evaporated Milk
1 oz. Sweetened Condensed
Milk
¼ oz. Grenadine

Combine all ingredients in a
blender with a scoop of ice.
Process until smooth. Top
with a sprinkle of ground
cinnamon.

Melon Colada
2 oz. Melon Liqueur
1 oz. Rum
5 oz. Pina Colada Mix

Combine all ingredients in a
blender with a scoop of ice.
Process until smooth.

Melon Daiquiri
1 oz. Melon Liqueur
½ oz. Light Rum
2 oz. Sour Mix

Combine all ingredients in a
blender with a scoop of ice.
Process until smooth.

Melon Jamaican
1 ½ oz. Kahlua
1 ½ oz. Myer's Dark Rum
1 ½ oz. Melon Liqueur
2 oz. Pina Colada Mix

Combine all ingredients in a
blender with a scoop of ice.
Process until smooth. Garnish
with a pineapple spear.

Melon Zinger
2 oz. Melon Liqueur
3 oz. Lemonade

Combine both ingredients in a
blender with a scoop of ice.
Process until smooth.

Mexican Bandit
2 oz. Tequila
2 oz. Peach Schnapps
2 oz. Lime Juice

Combine all ingredients in a
blender with a scoop of ice.
Process until smooth. Garnish
with a lime slice.

Mexican Blackberry
1 ½ oz. Tequila
1 oz. Blackberry Brandy
1 oz. Lemon Juice

Combine all ingredients in a
blender with a scoop of ice.
Process until smooth.

Mexican Zinger
1 ¼ oz. Tequila
½ oz. Lime Juice
¼ oz. Triple Sec`
2 scoops Vanilla Ice Cream

Combine all ingredients in a blender. Process until smooth.

Midnight Madness Margarita, Part 1
¾ oz. Cuervo Gold Tequila
¾ oz. Blue Curacao
1 ½ oz. Sour Mix

Combine all ingredients in a blender with a scoop of ice. Process until smooth.

Midnight Madness Margarita, Part 2
¾ oz. Cuervo Gold Tequila
¾ oz. Red Curacao
1 ½ oz. Sour Mix

Combine all ingredients in a blender with a scoop of ice. Process until smooth.

In a hurricane glass, pour together Part 1 and Part 2. Swirl with a bar spoon.

Midori Colada
1 oz. Rum
2 oz. Midori Melon Liqueur
1 oz. Coco Lopez
2 oz. Pineapple Juice

Combine all ingredients in a blender with a scoop of ice. Process until smooth.

Midori Cooler
1 oz. Midori Melon Liqueur
½ oz. Bacardi Light Rum
1 ½ oz. Pineapple Juice
2 oz. Coco Lopez

Combine all ingredients in a blender with a scoop of ice. Process until smooth.

Mint Chocolate Chip Ice Cream
1 oz. Vodka
½ oz. Light Creme de Cacao
½ oz. Rumple Minze
½ oz. Baileys Irish Cream
¼ oz. White Creme de Menthe
¼ oz. Kahlua

Combine all ingredients in a blender with a scoop of ice. Process until smooth.

Mint Icicles
¾ oz. Rum
¾ oz. Green Creme de Menthe
¾ oz. Light Creme de Cacao
1 oz. Pina Colada Mix
1 scoop Vanilla Ice Cream

Combine all ingredients in a blender. Process until smooth.

Minute Margarita
1 ½ oz. Tequila
1 oz. Triple Sec 3 oz. Limeade

Combine all ingredients in a blender with a scoop of ice. Process until smooth. Pour into a salt-rimmed margarita glass. Garnish with a lime wedge.

Minze de Menthe
1 oz. Rumple Minze
1 oz. White Creme de Menthe
1 oz. Cream
1 scoop Vanilla Ice Cream

Combine all ingredients in a blender. Process until smooth.

Mississippi Mud
1 ½ oz. Southern Comfort
1 ½ oz. Kahlua
2 scoops Vanilla Ice Cream

Combine all ingredients in a blender. Process until smooth. Top with shaved chocolate.

Mistic Runner
½ oz. Mistico
½ oz. Blackberry Brandy
½ oz. Creme de Banana
½ oz. Grenadine
½ oz. Lime Juice
2 oz. Fresh Strawberries

Combine all ingredients in a blender with a scoop of ice. Process until smooth.

Mistral
1 oz. Chambord
2 oz. Dry White Wine
2 oz. Frozen or Fresh Strawberries

Combine all ingredients in a blender with a scoop of ice. Process until smooth.

Mocha Colada
1 ½ oz. Coffee Liqueur
1 oz. Vodka
1 oz. Chocolate Syrup
1 ½ oz. Cream
2 oz. Coco Lopez

Combine all ingredients in a blender with a scoop of ice. Process until smooth.

Mochaccino Mint
¾ oz. Peppermint Schnapps
¾ oz. Light Creme de Cacao
1 ½ oz. Cold Cappuccino

Combine all ingredients in a blender with a scoop of ice. Process until smooth.

Monkey
1 ½ oz. Light Rum
1 oz. Cream
1 whole Ripe Banana
1 scoop Vanilla Ice Cream

Combine all ingredients in a blender. Process until smooth.

Monkey Up
1 oz. Vodka
1 oz. Peach Schnapps
1 oz. Pineapple Juice
½ of a Ripe Banana
10 Fresh Strawberries

Combine all ingredients in a blender with a scoop of ice. Process until smooth.

Monte Blanc
1 oz. Chambord
1 oz. Vodka
1 oz. Cream
1 scoop Vanilla Ice Cream

Combine all ingredients in a blender. Process until smooth.

Montego Margarita
1 ½ oz. Appleton Estate VX
½ oz. Triple Sec
1 oz. Sour Mix

Combine all ingredients in a blender with a scoop of ice. Process until smooth. Garnish with a lime slice.

Montmarte
1 oz. Chambord
1 oz. Coffee Liqueur
1 oz. Cream

Combine all ingredients in a blender with ½ scoop of ice. Process until smooth.

Moonbeam
¾ oz. Amaretto
¾ oz. Light Creme de Cacao
1 scoop Vanilla Ice Cream

Combine all ingredients in a blender. Process until smooth.

Moonblue
1 oz. Blue Curacao
1 oz. Rum
2 oz. Passion Fruit Juice
2 oz. Coco Lopez
½ oz. of a Ripe Banana
½ oz. of a peeled Mango

Pour blue curacao into the bottom of an empty hurricane glass. Combine remaining ingredients in a blender with a scoop of ice. Process until smooth. Slowly pour frozen mixture on top of the curacao in the glass.

Moose Milk
1 oz. Light Rum
1 oz. Kahlua
1 scoop Strawberry Ice Cream
1 oz. Frozen Strawberries

Combine all ingredients in a blender. Process until smooth. Garnish with a fresh strawberry.

Morganog
1 ½ oz. Captain Morgan Spiced Rum
1 scoop Vanilla Ice Cream

Combine both ingredients in a blender. Process until smooth. Top with a sprinkle of ground nutmeg.

Mud Slide
¾ oz. Baileys Irish Cream
¾ oz. Kahlua
¾ oz. Vodka
¾ oz. Cream
1 scoop Vanilla Ice Cream

Combine all ingredients in a
blender. Process until smooth.

Mush Melon
2 oz. Melon Liqueur
2 oz. Lemon Juice
1 oz. Honey

Combine all ingredients in a
blender with a scoop of ice.
Process until smooth.

Muskie Shake
2 oz. Creme de Banana
1 whole Ripe Banana
1 scoop Vanilla Ice Cream

Combine all ingredients in a
blender. Process until smooth.

Mustang Ranch Freebie
¾ oz. Rum
½ oz. Sour Mix
1 oz. Grapefruit Juice
¼ oz. Grenadine

Combine all ingredients in a
blender with ½ scoop of ice.
Process until smooth. Pour
into a champagne glass.

Neon Creeper
1 oz. Bacardi Limon Rum
1 oz. Absolut Citron
Vodka
1 oz. Midori Melon Liqueur
1 oz. Blue Curacao
1 oz. Triple Sec
2 oz. Sour Mix

Combine all ingredients in a
blender with a scoop of ice.
Process until smooth.
Pour into a hurricane glass.
Garnish with a lime wheel.

Nostalgia
½ oz. Cointreau
½ oz. Sweet Vermouth
½ oz. White Wine
½ oz. Creme de Banana
1 oz. Cream
½ of a Ripe Banana

Combine all ingredients in a
blender with a scoop of ice.
Process until smooth.

**Not Just Another Frozen
Drink**
1 oz. Grand Marnier
1 oz. Vodka
½ oz. Amaretto
¾ oz. each Pineapple Juice
¾ oz. Orange Juice
1 oz. Sour Mix

Combine all ingredients in a
blender with a scoop of ice.
Process until smooth. Top
with ¼ oz. cranberry juice.
Garnish with an orange slice
and a cherry.

Nutcracker Sweet
1 ½ oz. Amaretto
2 scoops Coffee Ice Cream

Combine both ingredients in a
blender. Process until smooth.
Top with whipped cream and
a sprinkle of nutmeg.

Nuthouse Delight
1 ½ oz. Kahlua
2 oz. Cream
1 scoop Vanilla Ice Cream
1 tbs. Peanut Butter

Combine all ingredients in a
blender. Process until smooth.

Nuts to You
¾ oz. Frangelico
¾ oz. Dark Creme de Cacao
¾ oz. Amaretto
2 oz. Cream

Combine all ingredients in a
blender with a scoop of ice.
Process until smooth.

Nutty Buddy
1 oz. Kahlua
1 oz. Frangelico
1 scoop Vanilla Ice Cream

Combine all ingredients in a
blender. Process until smooth.

Nutty Colada
3 oz. Amaretto
½ oz. Coco Lopez
1 oz. Crushed Pineapple

Combine all ingredients in a
blender with a scoop of ice.
Process until smooth.

Nutty Monkey
1 ¼ oz. Amaretto
1 ¼ oz. Creme de Banana

Combine both ingredients in a
blender with a scoop of ice.
Process until smooth.

Nutty Pina Colada
1 ½ oz. Amaretto
1 ½ oz. Gold Rum
1 ½ oz. Pineapple Juice
1 ½ oz. Coco Lopez

Combine all ingredients in a
blender with a scoop of ice.
Process until smooth. Garnish
with a pineapple chunk.

One Night Stand
2 oz. Tequila
1 oz. Light Rum
2 oz. Apple Juice
1 tsp. Sugar

Combine all ingredients in a
blender with a scoop of ice.
Process until smooth. Garnish
with a lime slice and a
pineapple chunk.

Ooh Baby Baby
1 oz. Amaretto
1 oz. Kahlua
4 oz. Pina Colada Mix

Combine all ingredients in a
blender with a scoop of ice.
Process until smooth.

Oral Fixation
1 oz. Dark Creme de Cacao
1 oz. Light Creme de Cacao
1 oz. Amaretto
2 oz. Pina Colada Mix

Combine all ingredients in a
blender with a scoop of ice.
Process until smooth.

Orange Blossom Special
1 oz. Peach Schnapps
2 oz. 7-Up
2 oz. Cream
1 scoop Vanilla Ice Cream
1 scoop Orange Sherbet

Combine all ingredients in a
blender. Process until smooth.
Garnish with an orange slice
and a cherry.

Orange Daiquiri
1 ½ oz. Bacardi Light Rum
½ oz. Lime Juice
1 oz. Orange Juice
1 tsp. Sugar

Combine all ingredients in a
blender with a scoop of ice.
Process until smooth.

Orange Olu
1 oz. Vodka
¾ oz. Cointreau
½ oz. Lime Juice
½ oz. Simple Syrup
1 Whole Ripe Peach

Combine all ingredients in a
blender with a scoop of ice.
Process until smooth. Top
with 2 oz. orange juice.
Garnish with an orange slice
and a cherry.

Orange Tree
1 ½ oz. Amaretto
¾ oz. Creme de Noyeaux
1 ½ oz. Orange Juice
1 scoop Vanilla Ice Cream

Combine all ingredients in a
blender. Process until smooth.
Top with whipped cream.
Garnish with an orange slice.

Oreo Speedwagon
2 oz. Kahlua
2 scoops Vanilla Ice Cream
3 Oreo Cookies

Combine all ingredients in a
blender. Process until smooth.
Top with whipped cream and
crushed Oreo cookies.

Over The Rainbow
2 oz. Spiced Rum
1 oz. Orange Curacao
2 scoops Rainbow Sherbet
½ of a Ripe Peach
2 Strawberries

Combine all ingredients in a
blender. Process until smooth.
Garnish with a fresh peach
slice and a strawberry.

P.S. I Love You
¾ oz. Baileys Irish Cream
¾ oz. Amaretto
¾ oz. Rum
¾ oz. Kahlua
1 scoop Vanilla Ice Cream

Combine all ingredients in a
blender. Process until smooth.

Pain in the Ass, Part 1
1 ½ oz. Rum
½ oz. Sour Mix
1 ½ oz. Strawberry Liqueur
½ oz. Grenadine

Combine all ingredients in a
blender with a scoop of ice.
Process until smooth.

Pain in the Ass, Part 2
1 ½ oz. Rum
1 ½ oz. Coco Lopez
3 oz. Pineapple Juice

Combine all ingredients in a
blender with a scoop of ice.
Process until smooth.

Carefully swirl together Part 1
with Part 2 in a hurricane
glass.

Palm Court
2 oz. Cuervo Gold Tequila
1 oz. Triple Sec
1 oz. Orange Juice

Combine all ingredients in a
blender with a scoop of ice.
Process until smooth. Garnish
with a lime wedge, a
pineapple spear, and a fresh
mint sprig.

Panda Bear
1 oz. Amaretto
½ oz. Light Creme de Cacao
½ oz. Dark Creme de Cacao
¼ oz. Chocolate Syrup
Dash of Vanilla Extract
1 scoop Vanilla Ice Cream

Combine all ingredients in a
blender. Process until smooth.

Papa John
2 oz. Light Rum
1 oz. Maraschino Liqueur
2 oz. Grapefruit Juice
Dash of Lime Juice
Dash of Lemon Juice

Combine all ingredients in a
blender with a scoop of ice.
Process until smooth.

**Paradise by the Dashboard
Lights**
1 oz. Dark Rum
1 oz. Light Rum
2 oz. Coco Lopez
½ of a Ripe Banana
1 Pineapple Slice
4 Cherries
1 scoop Vanilla Ice Cream

Combine all ingredients in a
blender. Process until smooth.
Top with whipped cream.

Passion Colada
2 ½ oz. Bacardi Amber Rum
1 oz. Coco Lopez
2 oz. Passion Fruit Nectar

Combine all ingredients in a
blender with a scoop of ice.
Process until smooth. Garnish
with a fresh mint leaf.

Patria Colada
1 oz. Bacardi Light Rum
3 oz. Coco Lopez
3 oz. Passion Fruit Nectar

Combine all ingredients in a
blender with a scoop of ice.
Process until smooth. Float ½
oz. Myer's Dark Rum on top.

Peach Blossom
1 ½ oz. Peach Schnapps
1 oz. Amaretto
1 scoop Vanilla Ice Cream

Combine all ingredients in a
blender. Process until smooth.

Peach Blow Fizz
1 oz. Gin
½ oz. Cream
¼ oz. Lemon Juice
1 tsp. Sugar
½ of a Ripe Peach

Combine all ingredients in a
blender with a few cubes of
ice. Process until smooth.
Top with a splash of club
soda.

Peach Cream
1 ½ oz. Peach Schnapps
¼ oz. Grenadine
2 scoops Vanilla Ice Cream
½ of an Apple, cut in chunks

Combine all ingredients in a
blender. Process until smooth.

Peach Daiquiri
3 oz. Bacardi Light Rum
1 oz. Sour Mix
1 tsp. Sugar
2 fresh Peach Halves

Combine all ingredients in a blender with a scoop of ice. Process until smooth. Garnish with a fresh peach slice.

Peach Frost
1 oz. Captain Morgan Spiced Rum
1 oz. Peach Schnapps
2 oz. Peach Puree

Combine all ingredients in a blender with a scoop of ice. Process until smooth. Garnish with an orange slice and a cherry.

Peach Fuzz
2 oz. Peach Schnapps
2 oz. Orange Juice
1 scoop Vanilla Ice Cream

Combine all ingredients in a blender. Process until smooth.

Peach Melba
1 oz. Peach Schnapps
1 oz. Raspberry Liqueur
1 oz. Cream
1 scoop Vanilla Ice Cream

Combine all ingredients in a blender. Process until smooth. Top with whipped cream.

Peach Melba Freeze
¾ oz. Peach Schnapps
¾ oz. Black Raspberry Liqueur
¾ oz. Hazelnut Liqueur
¾ oz. Cream
1 oz. Raspberry Jam
1 scoop Vanilla Ice Cream

Combine all ingredients in a blender. Process until smooth. Garnish with a fresh peach slice.

Peach Punch
½ oz. Captain Morgan Spiced Rum
½ oz. Peach Schnapps
2 oz. Pina Colada Mix
4 oz. Orange Juice

Combine all ingredients in a blender with a scoop of ice. Process until smooth. Garnish with a fresh peach slice.

Peaches & Cream
1 oz. Vodka
1 ¼ oz. Peach Schnapps
1 scoop Vanilla Ice Cream

Combine all ingredients in a blender with ½ scoop of ice. Process until smooth. Top with whipped cream.

Peachsicle
1 oz. Peach Schnapps
3 oz. Orange Juice
1 whole sliced Peach
1 scoop Vanilla Ice Cream

Combine all ingredients in a blender. Process until smooth. Top with whipped cream. Garnish with an orange slice.

Peachy Amaretto
2 oz. Amaretto
2 oz. Canned Peaches
1 scoop Vanilla Ice Cream

Combine all ingredients in a blender. Process until smooth. Garnish with a fresh peach slice.

Peachy Colada
½ oz. Captain Morgan Spiced Rum
¼ oz. Peach Schnapps
½ oz. Coco Lopez
4 oz. Pineapple Juice

Combine all ingredients in a blender with a scoop of ice. Process until smooth.

Peachy Keen
1 ½ oz. Peach Schnapps
1 oz. Cream
½ of a Ripe Peach
1 scoop Vanilla Ice Cream

Combine all ingredients in a blender. Process until smooth. Top with whipped cream and a cherry.

Peachy Orange Colada
1 ½ oz. Peach Schnapps
2 oz. Orange Juice
2 oz. Coco Lopez
½ oz. Grenadine

Combine all ingredients in a blender with a scoop of ice. Process until smooth.

Peachy Pina
1 ½ oz. Light Rum
2 oz. Pineapple Juice
1 oz. Coco Lopez
1 whole Peach, cut up

Combine all ingredients in a
blender with a scoop of ice.
Process until smooth. Garnish
with a pineapple wedge.

**Peanut Butter & Jelly
Freeze**
1 ½ oz. Grape Schnapps
1 Reese's Peanut Butter Cup
1 scoop Vanilla Ice Cream

Combine all ingredients in a
blender. Process until smooth.

Peanut Butter Cocktail
1 ½ oz. Kahlua
½ oz. Tequila
1 ½ oz. Cream
1 tbs. Peanut Butter

Combine all ingredients in a
blender with ½ scoop of ice.
Process until smooth.

Peanut Butter Cup
1 ½ oz. Dark Creme de Cacao
1 tbs. Peanut Butter
½ oz. Hershey's Syrup
1 scoop Vanilla Ice Cream

Combine all ingredients in a
blender. Process until smooth.
Top with whipped cream and
a cherry.

Peanut Butter Sundae
1 oz. Light Rum
½ oz. Amaretto
1 oz. Cream
¼ oz. Chocolate Syrup
2 scoops Vanilla Ice Cream

Combine all ingredients in a
blender. Process until smooth.
Top with whipped cream.

Pearls of Praline
1 ½ oz. Praline Liqueur
1 ½ oz. Pina Colada Mix
2 oz. Cream

Combine all ingredients in a
blender with a scoop of ice.
Process until smooth.

Pensacola
1 ½ oz. Light Rum
¼ oz. Guava Nectar
¼ oz. Lemon Juice
¼ oz. Orange Juice

Combine all ingredients in a
blender with ½ scoop of ice.
Process until smooth.

Peppar Southside
1 oz. Absolut Peppar Vodka
¼ oz. Lime Juice
2 tsp. Sugar
½ tsp. Fresh Mint Leaves

Combine all ingredients in a
blender with ½ scoop of ice.
Process until smooth. Garnish
with a slice of lime.

Peppermint Nightmare
2 oz. Peppermint Schnapps
2 oz. Cream
1 tbs. Peppermint Extract
2 scoops Vanilla Ice Cream

Combine all ingredients in a
blender. Process until smooth.
Pour into a hurricane glass
and top with ½ oz. vodka.

Peppermint Penguin
½ oz. Green Creme de
Menthe
½ oz. Chocolate Mint Liqueur
3 Oreo Cookies
3 oz. Cream

Combine all ingredients in a
blender with a scoop of ice.
Process until smooth. Top
with whipped cream and a
cherry.

Peppermint Twist
1 ½ oz. Peppermint Schnapps
½ oz. Light Creme de Cacao
2 scoops Vanilla Ice Cream

Combine all ingredients in a
blender. Process until smooth.
Garnish with a fresh mint
sprig and a miniature candy
cane.

Peppermint-Ade
1 ½ oz. Peppermint Schnapps
3 oz. Orange Juice
2 oz. Pineapple Juice

Combine all ingredients in a
blender with a scoop of ice.
Process until smooth. Garnish
with a fresh mint leaf and a
slice of lime.

Perfect Peach
1 oz. Peach Schnapps
1 oz. Gin
1 ½ oz. Orange Juice
1 ½ oz. Cranberry Juice

Combine all ingredients in a
blender with a scoop of ice.
Process until smooth.

Petting Zoo
1 oz. Wild Turkey
1 oz. White Horse Scotch
1 oz. El Toro Tequila
1 oz. Rum
4 oz. Gatorade

Combine all ingredients in a
blender with a scoop of ice.
Process until smooth.

Picador
1 ½ oz. White Tequila
3 oz. Pineapple Juice
½ oz. Lime Juice

Combine all ingredients in a
blender with a scoop of ice.
Process until smooth. Garnish
with a pineapple stick.

Pier Milkshake Heaven
½ oz. Godiva Chocolate
Liqueur
½ oz. Baileys Irish Cream
¾ oz. Butterscotch Schnapps
¼ oz. Cream
1 scoop Vanilla Ice Cream

Combine all ingredients in a
blender. Process until smooth.
Top with whipped cream and
a sprinkle of cocoa powder.

Pina Colada
1 ½ oz. Rum
1 ½ oz. Coco Lopez
3 oz. Pineapple Juice

Combine all ingredients in a
blender with a scoop of ice.
Process until smooth.
Garnish with a pineapple
chunk and a cherry.

Pina Colada Freeze
1 ½ oz. Malibu Rum
2 oz. Coco Lopez
3 oz. Crushed Pineapple
2 scoops Vanilla Ice Cream

Combine all ingredients in a
blender. Process until smooth.

Pina Fria
2 oz. Light Rum
3 oz. Pineapple Juice
2 oz. Lemon Juice
3 Canned Pineapple Slices
6 Fresh Mint Sprigs

Combine all ingredients in a
blender with a scoop of ice.
Process until smooth.

Pina-Banana Freeze
1 ¼ oz. Pina Colada Schnapps
½ oz. Creme de Banana
1 oz. Coco Lopez
1 oz. Pineapple Juice

Combine all ingredients in a
blender with a scoop of ice.
Process until smooth. Garnish
with a pineapple slice.

Pinata
1 ½ oz. White Tequila
1 oz. Lime Juice
½ oz. Creme de Banana

Combine all ingredients in a
blender with a scoop of ice.
Process until smooth.

Pineapple Banana Refresher
1 oz. Dark Rum
1 oz. Creme de Banana
2 oz. Pineapple Juice
1 scoop Pineapple Sherbet

Combine all ingredients in a
blender. Process until smooth.
Garnish with a pineapple
wedge and a banana slice.

Pineapple Daiquiri
2 oz. Bacardi Light Rum
1 slice Canned Pineapple
¼ oz. Lime Juice
1 tsp. Sugar

Combine all ingredients in a
blender with a scoop of ice.
Process until smooth.

Pineberry Smash
1 ½ oz. Chambord
½ oz. Vodka
1 oz. Triple Sec
2 oz. Pineapple Juice
3 oz. Sour Mix
3 slices Canned Pineapple

Combine all ingredients in a
blender with a scoop of ice.
Process until smooth.

Pink Orchid
1 ¼ oz. Captain Morgan
Spiced Rum
2 oz. Cranberry Juice
2 oz. Pineapple Juice
¼ oz. Coco Lopez

Combine all ingredients in a
blender with a scoop of ice.
Process until smooth. Garnish
with a fresh mint leaf.

Pino Frio
1 ¼ oz. Myer's Dark Rum
2 Slices Canned Pineapple
1 tsp. Sugar

Combine all ingredients in a
blender with a scoop of ice.
Process until smooth.
Garnish with a cherry.

Pirate's Spyglass
1 oz. Captain Morgan Spiced
Rum
1 tbs. Honey
½ oz. Cream
2 scoops Vanilla Ice Cream

Combine all ingredients in a
blender. Process until smooth.

Pistachio Cream
1 oz. Pistachio Liqueur
1 oz. Brandy
1 scoop Vanilla Ice Cream

Combine all ingredients in a
blender. Process until smooth.

Pistachio Mint Ice Cream
1 oz. Frangelico
1 oz. Vodka
½ oz. Green Creme de
Menthe
2 oz. Cream
1 scoop Vanilla Ice Cream

Combine all ingredients in a
blender. Process until smooth.
Garnish with a fresh mint leaf.

Polar Bear
¾ oz. Kahlua
¾ oz. Vodka
1 scoop Vanilla Ice Cream

Combine all ingredients in a
blender. Process until smooth.
Top with whipped cream.

Poolside
1 oz. Strawberry Schnapps
1 oz. Vodka
5 oz. Lemonade
2 oz. Fresh Strawberries

Combine all ingredients in a
blender with a scoop of ice.
Process until smooth.

Pornodog
2 oz. Vodka
3 oz. Apple Juice
3 oz. Fresh Strawberries

Combine all ingredients in a
blender with a scoop of ice.
Process until smooth. Garnish
with a fresh strawberry.

Princess' Pleasure
1 oz. Peach Schnapps
2 oz. Pineapple Juice
2 oz. Coco Lopez
½ of a Ripe Banana

Combine all ingredients in a
blender with a scoop of ice.
Process until smooth. Garnish
with a cherry.

Pucker Up
1 ½ oz. Sour Apple Pucker
Schnapps
¾ oz. Vodka
2 scoops Vanilla Ice Cream

Combine all ingredients in a
blender. Process until smooth.

Pug Juice
1 oz. Vodka
1 oz. Grain Alcohol
2 oz. Grape Kool-Aid
2 oz. Pineapple Juice
2 scoops Rainbow Sherbet

Combine all ingredients in a
blender. Process until smooth.

Puppet
2 oz. Absolut Citron Vodka
2 oz. Orange Juice
2 oz. 7-Up

Combine all ingredients in a
blender with a scoop of ice.
Process until smooth.

Purple Parrot
1 oz. Dark Rum
1 oz. Baileys Irish Cream
2 oz. Pineapple Juice
2 oz. Coco Lopez

Combine all ingredients in a blender with a scoop of ice. Process until smooth.

Purple Smurf
1 oz. Vodka
1 oz. Strawberry Schnapps
1 oz. Blueberry Schnapps
1 oz. Sloe Gin
2 oz. Lemonade

Combine all ingredients in a blender with a scoop of ice. Process until smooth.

Push-Up
1 oz. Vodka
2 oz. Orange Juice
½ oz. Cream
Dash of Grenadine
1 scoop Vanilla Ice Cream

Combine all ingredients in a blender. Process until smooth.

Quicksand
1 ½ oz. Vodka
1 ½ oz. Coffee Liqueur
3 oz. Cream
½ oz. Hershey's Syrup
3 tbs. Ovaltine Powder

Combine all ingredients in a blender with a scoop of ice. Process until smooth. Top with whipped cream and a cherry.

Ragtop
1 ½ oz. Bacardi 151 Rum
½ oz. Lime Juice
5 oz. Fresh Watermelon
(seeds removed)

Combine all ingredients in a blender with a scoop of ice. Process until smooth. Garnish with a watermelon cube.

Rainbow Reef
½ oz. Bacardi Light Rum
½ oz. Amaretto
¼ oz. Midori Melon Liqueur
¼ oz. Blue Curacao
¼ oz. Grenadine
1 oz. Pina Colada Mix

Combine Rum, Amaretto, & Pina Colada mix in a blender with a scoop of ice. Process until smooth. Pour Grenadine in bottom of a hurricane glass. Pour in ½ of the frozen mix into the glass. Add Blue Curacao. Fill with remaining frozen drink.

Raspberries & Cream
1 ¼ oz. Raspberry Liqueur
1 ¼ oz. Cream
1 tbs. Sugar
¼ cup Fresh Raspberries

Combine all ingredients in a blender with a scoop of ice. Process until smooth. Garnish with a fresh raspberry.

Raspberry Banana Split, Part 1
1 oz. Kahlua
1 scoop Vanilla Ice Cream

Combine both ingredients in a blender. Process until smooth.

Raspberry Banana Split, Part 2
1 oz. Creme de Banana
1 scoop Vanilla Ice Cream

Combine both ingredients in a blender. Process until smooth.

Raspberry Banana Split, Part 3
1 oz. Chambord
1 scoop Vanilla Ice Cream

Combine both ingredients in a blender. Process until smooth.

In a hurricane glass, carefully layer Parts 1, 2, & 3. Top with whipped cream.

Raspberry Brownie
1 oz. Kahlua
1 oz. Chambord
1 scoop Vanilla Ice Cream

Combine all ingredients in a blender. Process until smooth.

Raspberry Cheesecake
1 oz. Black Raspberry Liqueur
1 oz. Light Creme de Cacao
½ oz. Softened Cream Cheese
2 scoops Vanilla Ice Cream

Combine all ingredients in a blender with ½ scoop of ice. Process until smooth.

Raspberry Colada
1 ½ oz. Raspberry Schnapps
½ oz. Rum
3 oz. Pina Colada Mix
Dash of Grenadine

Combine all ingredients in a blender with a scoop of ice. Process until smooth. Garnish with a fresh raspberry.

Raspberry Cream
1 oz. Vodka
½ oz. Light Creme de Cacao
1 oz. Cream
1 tbs. Vanilla Yogurt
1 scoop Vanilla Ice Cream

Combine all ingredients in a blender. Process until smooth.

Raspberry Margarita
1 oz. Cuervo Gold Tequila
½ oz. Grand Marnier
½ oz. Chambord
½ cup Fresh Raspberries
1 ½ oz. Sour Mix

Combine all ingredients in a blender with a scoop of ice. Process until smooth. Pour into a sugar-rimmed hurricane glass.

Raspberry Mudslide
¾ oz. Kahlua
¾ oz. Vodka
¾ oz. Baileys Irish Cream
¾ oz. Chambord
1 scoop Vanilla Ice Cream

Combine all ingredients in a blender. Process until smooth.

Raspberry Popsicle
¾ oz. Raspberry Schnapps
¾ oz. Rum
¾ oz. Sour Mix
½ oz. Lime Juice
¼ oz. Grenadine

Combine all ingredients in a blender with a scoop of ice. Process until smooth.

Raspberry Royale
1 oz. Chambord
1 oz. Rum
1 scoop Vanilla Ice Cream

Combine all ingredients in a blender. Process until smooth.

Raspberry Sherbet
2 oz. Chambord
1 oz. Coco Lopez
2 oz. Pineapple Juice

Combine all ingredients in a blender with a scoop of ice. Process until smooth.

Raspberry Sorbet
1 oz. Chambord
¾ oz. Malibu Rum
1 oz. Absolut Vodka
2 oz. Cranberry Juice
1 ½ oz. Sour Mix
1 oz. Grapefruit Juice

Combine all ingredients in a blender with a scoop of ice. Process until smooth.

Raspberry Sparkler
2 oz. Champagne
3 oz. Champagne
2 oz. Raspberry Puree

Combine all ingredients in a blender with a scoop of ice. Process until smooth.

Raspberry Tequila
2 oz. White Tequila
2 oz. Chambord

Combine both ingredients in a blender with a scoop of ice. Process until smooth. Pour into a salt-rimmed cocktail glass.

Razzaccino Mudslide
¾ oz. Baileys Irish Cream
¾ oz. Vodka
¾ oz. Kahlua
¾ oz. Raspberry Schnapps
1 oz. Cold Cappuccino

Combine all ingredients in a blender with a scoop of ice. Process until smooth.

Razzbaretto
1 ¼ oz. Amaretto
1 ¼ oz. Black Raspberry Liqueur
1 scoop Vanilla Ice Cream

Combine all ingredients in a blender. Process until smooth.

Razzberita Punch
1 ½ oz. Raspberry Schnapps
½ oz. Tequila
2 oz. Limeade
2 oz. 7-Up
1 scoop Raspberry Sherbet

Combine all ingredients in a
blender. Process until smooth.

Razz-Ma-Tazz
1 oz. Brandy
¾ oz. Black Raspberry
Liqueur 2 oz. Cream

Combine all ingredients in a
blender with a scoop of ice.
Process until smooth.

Reggae Ambassador
2 oz. Absolut Citron Vodka
3 oz. Pine-Orange-Banana
Juice
2 oz. Fresh Strawberries
1 tbs. Sugar

Combine all ingredients in a
blender with a scoop of ice.
Process until smooth. Garnish
with an orange slice.

Reindeer Milk
1 ½ oz. Peppermint Schnapps
1 oz. Bourbon
3 oz. Cream

Combine all ingredients in a
blender with a scoop of ice.
Process until smooth. Top
with a sprinkle of ground
nutmeg.

Rendez-Vous
1 ½ oz. Amaretto di Saronno
½ oz. Light Rum
1 ½ oz. Pineapple Juice
½ oz. Coco Lopez

Combine all ingredients in a
blender with a scoop of ice.
Process until smooth. Garnish
with a pineapple slice and a
cherry.

Reunion
½ oz. White Sambuca
½ oz. Vodka
½ oz. Strawberry Liqueur
3 oz. Orange Juice
6 fresh Strawberries

Combine all ingredients in a
blender with a scoop of ice.
Process until smooth.

Road Runner
1 ½ oz. Vodka
¾ oz. Amaretto
¾ oz. Coco Lopez

Combine all ingredients in a
blender with a scoop of ice.
Process until smooth. Garnish
with an orange slice and a
sprinkle of ground nutmeg.

Roiano Daiquiri
¾ oz. Liquore Roiano
¾ oz. Light Rum
Juice of ½ Lime
1 tsp. Powdered Sugar

Combine all ingredients in a
blender with a scoop of ice.
Process until smooth.

Roman Cow
2 oz. White Sambuca
3 oz. Rum
1 oz. Lemon Juice
1 whole Ripe Banana
1 raw Egg

Combine all ingredients in a
blender with a scoop of ice.
Process until smooth.
Garnish with a cherry.

Roman Frullati
3 oz. Gin
2 oz. Diced Apples
2 oz. Diced Pears
2 oz. Canned Peaches
1 oz. Maraschino Liqueur
1 oz. Almond Extract

Combine all ingredients in a
blender with a scoop of ice.
Process until smooth.

Root Beer Shake
1 ¼ oz. Root Beer Schnapps
1 oz. Coco Lopez
½ of a Ripe Banana
Splash of Club Soda

Combine all ingredients in a
blender with a scoop of ice.
Process until smooth. Garnish
with a cherry.

Root Canal
¾ oz. Root Beer Schnapps
¾ oz. Light Creme de Cacao
½ oz. Hershey's Syrup
1 scoop Vanilla Ice Cream

Combine all ingredients in a
blender. Process until smooth.

Roseanne Bananadana
1 ½ oz. Cuervo Gold Tequila
½ oz. Cream
¼ oz. Licor 43
½ of a Ripe Banana
Dash of Ground Cinnamon

Combine all ingredients in a blender with a scoop of ice. Process until smooth. Garnish with a banana slice.

Rose's Colada
1 ½ oz. Light Rum
1 oz. Lime Juice
1 oz. Coco Lopez
3 oz. Pineapple Juice

Combine all ingredients in a blender with a scoop of ice. Process until smooth.

Rose's Pineapple Daiquiri
1 ¼ oz. Light Rum
¼ oz. Triple Sec
¾ oz. Lime Juice
3 oz. Pineapple Juice

Combine all ingredients in a blender with a scoop of ice. Process until smooth.

Rose's Strawberry Margarita
¾ oz. Tequila
½ oz. Triple Sec
1 oz. Lime Juice
½ cup Fresh Strawberries

Combine all ingredients in a blender with a scoop of ice. Process until smooth. Pour into a sugar-rimmed margarita glass. Garnish with a lime wheel and a strawberry.

Rosy Frozen Punch
1 ½ oz. Peach Schnapps
½ oz. Triple Sec
1 ½ oz. Sour Mix
¼ oz. Grenadine

Combine all ingredients in a blender with a scoop of ice. Process until smooth.

Royal Dream
1 ¼ oz. Chambord
3 oz. Pina Colada Mix
1 scoop Vanilla Ice Cream

Combine all ingredients in a blender. Process until smooth.

Royal Hummer
¾ oz. Baileys Irish Cream
¾ oz. Amaretto
1 scoop Vanilla Ice Cream

Combine all ingredients in a blender. Process until smooth.

Royal Peach Freeze
2 oz. Peach Schnapps
1 ½ oz. Sparkling White Wine
½ oz. Lime Juice
2 oz. Orange Juice

Combine all ingredients in a blender with a scoop of ice. Process until smooth.

Rubicon
1 oz. Jack Daniel's
2 oz. Lemon-Lime Kool-Aid
½ oz. Lemon-Lime Gatorade
2 scoops Vanilla Ice Cream
1 tsp. Butter

Combine all ingredients in a blender. Process until smooth.

Ruffler
2 oz. Baileys Irish Cream
1 oz. Vodka
2 tbs. Hot Chocolate Mix
1 tsp. Instant Coffee Powder
1 oz. Cream

Combine all ingredients in a blender with a scoop of ice. Process until smooth.

Rum Honey
2 oz. Bacardi 151 Rum
2 oz. Lemon Juice
2 tbs. Honey

Combine all ingredients in a blender with a scoop of ice. Process until smooth.

Rum Nut
1 oz. Light Rum
½ oz. Kahlua
2 oz. Coco Lopez
1 scoop Vanilla Ice Cream

Combine all ingredients in a blender. Process until smooth.

Rum Runner
1 oz. Bacardi Light Rum
½ oz. Blackberry Brandy
½ oz. Creme de Banana
½ oz. Sour Mix
½ oz. Pineapple Juice
½ oz. Grenadine

Combine all ingredients in a blender with a scoop of ice. Process until smooth. Float ½ oz. Bacardi 151 Rum on top.

Rummy Sour
1 ¼ oz. Captain Morgan
Spiced Rum
1 ½ oz. Sour Mix
¼ oz. Lime Juice

Combine all ingredients in a
blender with a scoop of ice.
Process until smooth.

Russian Coffee
1 oz. Vodka
1 oz. Kahlua
1 oz. Cream
2 oz. Cold Coffee

Combine all ingredients in a
blender with a scoop of ice.
Process until smooth.

Russian Dream
1 oz. Stolichnaya Vodka
1 oz. Baileys Irish Cream
1 oz. Cream

Combine all ingredients in a
blender with a scoop of ice.
Process until smooth.

Rusty Anchor
1 ½ oz. Kahlua
1 ½ oz. Myer's Dark Rum
4 oz. Coco Lopez
½ of a Ripe Banana

Combine all ingredients in a
blender with a scoop of ice.
Process until smooth. Top
with whipped cream.

S.W.S
2 oz. Strawberry Schnapps
2 oz. Triple Sec
1 ½ oz. Tonic Water

Combine all ingredients in a
blender with a scoop of ice.
Process until smooth.

Saigon Girl
1 oz. Vodka
¾ oz. Midori Melon Liqueur
½ oz. Blue Curacao
½ oz. Orange Juice
½ oz. Lemon Juice

Combine all ingredients in a
blender with ½ scoop of ice.
Process until smooth.

Salty Reindeer
1 oz. Tequila
1 oz. Triple Sec
2 oz. Orange Juice
1 oz. Rum

Combine all ingredients in a
blender with a scoop of ice.
Process until smooth. Pour
into a salt-rimmed margarita
glass. Garnish with an orange
slice and a cherry.

Sambucaccino
1 ½ oz. White Sambuca
2 oz. Cold Cappuccino

Combine both ingredients in a
blender with a scoop of ice.
Process until smooth.

Sand Pail
1 ¼ oz. Baileys Irish Cream
½ oz. Light Creme de Cacao
2 oz. Cream
1 oz. Chocolate Syrup
1 scoop Vanilla Ice Cream

Combine all ingredients in a
blender. Process until smooth.

Sanibel Breeze
¾ oz. Malibu Rum
¾ oz. Creme de Banana
¾ oz. Midori Melon Liqueur
¾ oz. Sour Mix
2 oz. Cranberry Juice
2 oz. Orange Juice
Dash of Grenadine

Combine all ingredients in a
blender with a scoop of ice.
Process until smooth.

Santarita
1 ½ oz. Cuervo White Tequila
1 oz. Triple Sec
2 oz. Cranberry Juice
1 oz. Lime Juice

Combine all ingredients in a
blender with a scoop of ice.
Process until smooth. Garnish
with a lime wheel.

Saronnada
1 ½ oz. Amaretto di Saronno
½ oz. Vodka
1 oz. Coco Lopez
2 oz. Pineapple Juice

Combine all ingredients in a
blender with a scoop of ice.
Process until smooth. Garnish
with a cherry.

Sauzaliky
2 oz. Sauza Tequila
4 oz. Orange Juice
Dash of Lemon Juice
1 whole Ripe Banana

Combine all ingredients in a blender with a scoop of ice. Process until smooth.

Savannah Banana
1 oz. Creme de Banana
¾ oz. Southern Comfort
¾ oz. Dark Creme de Cacao
1 scoop Vanilla Ice Cream

Combine all ingredients in a blender. Process until smooth. Top with whipped cream and a banana slice.

Scarlet Abyss
1 oz. Dry Vermouth
½ oz. Light Rum
1 ½ oz. Ginger Ale
2 oz. Cranberry Juice

Combine all ingredients in a blender with a scoop of ice. Process until smooth.

Schnaaplada
2 oz. Schnaapple
1 oz. Rum
4 oz. Pina Colada Mix

Combine all ingredients in a blender with a scoop of ice. Process until smooth.

Schnappin' Strawberries
1 ¼ oz. Strawberry Schnapps
1 oz. Pineapple Juice
1 oz. Coco Lopez
¼ cup Fresh Strawberries

Combine all ingredients in a blender with a scoop of ice. Process until smooth.

Screaming Epsilon
2 oz. Vodka
3 oz. Orange Juice
1 Egg White
1 tsp. Vanilla Extract

Combine all ingredients in a blender with a scoop of ice. Process until smooth.

Screwy Gator
1 ½ oz. Light Rum
2 oz. Orange Juice
2 oz. Orange Gatorade

Combine all ingredients in a blender with a scoop of ice. Process until smooth.

Sea Side Liberty
1 oz. Light Rum
¾ oz. Coffee Liqueur
1 oz. Coco Lopez
3 oz. Pineapple Juice
¼ oz. Cream

Combine all ingredients in a blender with a scoop of ice. Process until smooth. Garnish with a thin pineapple wedge.

Seductive Chocolate Raspberry
1 ¼ oz. Godiva Chocolate Liqueur
¾ oz. Chambord
1 scoop Vanilla Ice Cream

Combine all ingredients in a blender. Process until smooth. Top with whipped cream, a drizzle of chocolate syrup, chocolate shavings and a fresh raspberry.

Segne
1 oz. Coffee Liqueur
1 oz. Light Rum
2 scoops Vanilla Ice Cream

Combine all ingredients in a blender. Process until smooth.

Seville Strawberry Delight
½ oz. Light Creme de Cacao
½ oz. Amaretto
3 oz. Frozen Strawberries
1 scoop Vanilla Ice Cream

Combine all ingredients in a blender. Process until smooth. Garnish with a fresh strawberry.

Sex in the Arctic
1 ½ oz. Light Rum
1 oz. Pineapple Juice
1 oz. Orange Juice
1 oz. Cranberry Juice
1 scoop Strawberry Ice Cream

Combine all ingredients in a blender with a scoop of ice. Process until smooth.

Sex on the Rug
1 ½ oz. Bourbon
1 ½ oz. Kahlua
2 oz. Cream

Combine all ingredients in a
blender with a scoop of ice.
Process until smooth.

Sex Wax
1 oz. Light Rum
½ oz. Southern Comfort
1 oz. Orange Juice
1 oz. Pineapple Juice
1 oz. Coco Lopez

Combine all ingredients in a
blender with a scoop of ice.
Process until smooth.

Sex with a Virgin
2 oz. Butterscotch Schnapps
1 ½ oz. Baileys Irish Cream
1 oz. White Creme de Menthe
2 scoops Vanilla Ice Cream

Combine all ingredients in a
blender. Process until smooth.

Shamu
¾ oz. Chambord
¾ oz. Malibu Rum
2 oz. Pina Colada Mix

Combine all ingredients in a
blender with a scoop of ice.
Process until smooth.

Shipwreck
1 ¼ oz. Malibu Rum
1 ¼ oz. Creme de Banana
1 oz. Pina Colada Mix
1 scoop Vanilla Ice Cream

Combine all ingredients in a
blender. Process until smooth.

Silverbell
1 oz. Light Creme de Cacao
1 oz. Coco Lopez
2 oz. Pineapple Juice
1 oz. Cream

Combine all ingredients in a
blender with a scoop of ice.
Process until smooth.

Slalom
1 oz. Vodka
1 oz. Light Creme de Cacao
1 oz. White Sambuca
½ oz. Cream

Combine all ingredients in a
blender with a scoop of ice.
Process until smooth.

Slapstick
¾ oz. Captain Morgan Spiced
Rum
½ oz. Strawberry Liqueur
1 oz. Coco Lopez
1 oz. Grenadine
2 oz. Pineapple Juice

Combine all ingredients in a
blender with a scoop of ice.
Process until smooth.

Sloe Creme Soda
1 ½ oz. Sloe Gin
½ oz. Creme de Cassis
2 oz. Club Soda
2 scoops Vanilla Ice Cream

Combine all ingredients in a
blender. Process until smooth.
Garnish with a cherry.

Slow Gray
2 oz. Crown Royal
2 oz. Cream
2 scoops Vanilla Ice Cream

Combine all ingredients in a
blender. Process until smooth.
Garnish with a fresh mint leaf.

Slushy Hanky
1 oz. Godiva Chocolate
Liqueur
1 oz. Baileys Irish Cream
1 oz. Malibu Rum

Combine all ingredients in a
blender with a scoop of ice.
Process until smooth.

Smooth Move
1 oz. Rum
2 oz. Prune Juice
2 oz. Pineapple Juice
2 oz. Sour Mix

Combine all ingredients in a
blender with a scoop of ice.
Process until smooth. Garnish
with a pineapple spear and a
cherry.

Sneaky Pete
1 ½ oz. Malibu Rum
1 oz. Pina Colada Mix
1 oz. Orange Juice
1 oz. Pineapple Juice
½ oz. Grenadine

Combine all ingredients in a
blender with a scoop of ice.
Process until smooth.

Snow Bear
1 ½ oz. Amaretto
½ oz. Licor 43
1 oz. Cream
1 scoop Vanilla Ice Cream

Combine all ingredients in a
blender. Process until smooth.
Top with whipped cream and
a cherry.

Snow Cone
1 ¼ oz. Midori Melon Liqueur
¾ oz. Vodka
¾ oz. Amaretto
1 ½ oz. Orange Juice
½ oz. Sour Mix

Combine all ingredients in a
blender with a scoop of ice.
Process until smooth.

Snowball
1 ½ oz. Rumple Minze
1 ½ oz. Cream
1 scoop Vanilla Ice Cream

Combine all ingredients in a
blender with ½ scoop of ice.
Process until smooth.

Snowstorm
2 oz. Vodka
4 Slices Lemon
4 Slices Lime
2 tbs. Sugar

Combine all ingredients in a
blender with a scoop of ice.
Process until smooth.

Soiled BVDs
1 ½ oz. Peppermint Schnapps
1 oz. Vodka
2 scoops Chocolate Ice Cream

Combine all ingredients in a
blender. Process until smooth.

South of the Border
¾ oz. Orange Curacao
1 oz. Tequila
3 oz. Orange Juice
½ oz. Sour Mix
Dash of Grenadine

Combine all ingredients in a
blender with a scoop of ice.
Process until smooth.

Southern Peach
1 ½ oz. Bourbon
Dash of Grenadine
1 oz. Peach Schnapps
2 oz. Sour Mix
2 oz. Orange Juice

In a hurricane glass, combine
first two ingredients with ice.
Combine remaining
ingredients in a blender with
½ scoop ice. Process until
smooth. Pour frozen drink
into glass on top of first
ingredients.

**Sparkling Strawberry
Mimosa**
2 oz. Orange Juice
2 oz. Frozen Strawberries
4 oz. Chilled Champagne

Combine orange juice and
strawberries in a blender.
Process until smooth. Pour
into a large wine glass, and
fill with champagne. Garnish
with a strawberry and an
orange slice.

SpecOps
2 oz. Bombay Sapphire Gin
1 oz. Triple Sec
2 oz. Pineapple Juice

Combine all ingredients in a
blender with a scoop of ice.
Process until smooth. Garnish
with a pineapple slice.

SPF 15
2 oz. Kahlua
1 oz. Malibu Rum
3 oz. Cream
1 whole Ripe Banana

Combine all ingredients in a
blender with a scoop of ice.
Process until smooth.

Spiced Banana Daiquiri
1 oz. Captain Morgan Spiced
Rum
¼ oz. Creme de Banana
2 oz. Sour Mix
½ of a Ripe Banana

Combine all ingredients in a
blender with a scoop of ice.
Process until smooth. Garnish
with a banana slice and a
cherry.

Spiced Pina Colada
1 ½ oz. Captain Morgan
Spiced Rum
1 oz. Coco Lopez
4 oz. Pineapple Juice

Combine all ingredients in a
blender with a scoop of ice.
Process until smooth.
Garnish with a pineapple
spear and a cherry.

Splashdown Countdown

1 ½ oz. Vodka
3 oz. V-8 Splash
1 scoop Vanilla Ice Cream

Combine all ingredients in a blender. Process until smooth. Top with whipped cream.

Spring Breaker

2 oz. Vodka
½ oz. Triple Sec
2 oz. Sunny Delight Orange Drink
1 oz. Passion Fruit Juice

Combine all ingredients in a blender with a scoop of ice. Process until smooth. Top with a splash of ginger ale.

Spyglass

1 oz. Captain Morgan Spiced Rum
1 tbs. Honey
½ oz. Cream
2 scoops Vanilla Ice Cream

Combine all ingredients in a blender. Process until smooth.

Steppes

1 ½ oz. Vodka
1 oz. Dark Creme de Cacao
½ oz. Light Creme de Cacao
2 scoops Vanilla Ice Cream

Combine all ingredients in a blender. Process until smooth.

Storm Trooper

1 oz. Butterscotch Schnapps
½ oz. Baileys Irish Cream
½ oz. Black Sambuca
2 oz. Cream

Combine all ingredients in a blender with a scoop of ice. Process until smooth. Drizzle a bit of chocolate syrup on the inside of a hurricane glass and pour frozen drink into the middle.

Strametto Colada

1 ½ oz. Strawberry Schnapps
1 ½ oz. Amaretto
3 oz. Pina Colada Mix

Combine all ingredients in a blender with a scoop of ice. Process until smooth.

Strawbalada

1 ¼ oz. Cuervo Gold Tequila
¾ oz. Pina Colada Mix
1 tsp. Lemon Juice
¼ oz. Grenadine
½ cup Frozen or Fresh Strawberries

Combine all ingredients in a blender with a scoop of ice. Process until smooth. Garnish with a fresh strawberry.

Strawberries & Cream

2 oz. Strawberry Liqueur
2 oz. Fresh Strawberries
1 scoop Vanilla Ice Cream

Combine all ingredients in a blender. Process until smooth.

Strawberry Alexandra

1 oz. Brandy
1 oz. Light Creme de Cacao
5 oz. Fresh Strawberries
1 scoop Vanilla Ice Cream

Combine all ingredients in a blender. Process until smooth. Top with whipped cream and chocolate shavings.

Strawberry Banana Colada

1 ½ oz. Rum
2 oz. Coco Lopez
2 oz. Strawberries
1 medium Ripe Banana

Combine all ingredients in a blender with a scoop of ice. Process until smooth.

Strawberry Banana Spritz

1 ½ oz. Creme de Banana
2 oz. Fresh Strawberries
2 oz. Club Soda
1 scoop Vanilla Ice Cream

Combine all ingredients in a blender. Process until smooth. Garnish with a fresh strawberry.

Strawberry Cappuccino Rum Shake

1 oz. Myer's Dark Rum
½ oz. Dark Creme de Cacao
½ oz. Cold Cappuccino
2 oz. Frozen Strawberries
2 scoops Vanilla Ice Cream

Combine all ingredients in a blender. Process until smooth.

Strawberry Coco Ribe
2 oz. CocoRibe Rum
1 oz. Sour Mix
½ oz. Lime Juice
1 tbs. Sugar
10 Strawberries

Combine all ingredients in a blender with a scoop of ice. Process until smooth. Garnish with a strawberry.

Strawberry Colada
1 oz. Light Rum
1 oz. Dark Rum
1 ½ oz. Coco Lopez
3 oz. Pineapple Juice
6 Fresh Strawberries

Combine all ingredients in a blender with a scoop of ice. Process until smooth. Garnish with a pineapple slice and a strawberry.

Strawberry Daiquiri #1
1 ½ oz. Rum
½ oz. Sour Mix
1 ½ oz. Strawberry Liqueur
½ oz. Grenadine

Combine all ingredients in a blender with a scoop of ice. Process until smooth.

Strawberry Daiquiri #2
1 ½ oz. Bacardi Light Rum
¼ oz. Lime Juice
1 tsp. Sugar
3 oz. Fresh or Frozen Strawberries

Combine all ingredients in a blender with a scoop of ice. Process until smooth.

Strawberry Dawn
1 oz. Gin
1 oz. Coco Lopez
4 Fresh Strawberries

Combine all ingredients in a blender with ½ scoop of ice. Process until smooth. Garnish with a strawberry slice and a fresh mint sprig.

Strawberry Iced Tea
½ oz. Rum
½ oz. Vodka
½ oz. Gin
½ oz. Triple Sec
1 oz. Sour Mix
2 oz. Frozen Strawberries

Combine all ingredients in a blender with a scoop of ice. Process until smooth. Top with a dash of whipped cream and a fresh strawberry.

Strawberry Mudslide
¾ oz. Kahlua
¾ oz. Vodka
¾ oz. Baileys Irish Cream
¾ oz. Strawberry Liqueur
1 scoop Vanilla Ice Cream

Combine all ingredients in a blender. Process until smooth.

Strawberry Schmoe
1 ½ oz. Vodka
1 oz. Amaretto
1 oz. Sloe Gin 1 tbs. Sugar
3 oz. Fresh Strawberries

Combine all ingredients in a blender with ½ scoop of ice. Process until smooth.

Strawberry Shake
2 oz. Strawberry Schnapps
1 oz. Cream
1 raw Egg
1 scoop Vanilla Ice Cream

Combine all ingredients in a blender with a scoop of ice. Process until smooth. Top with whipped cream and a cherry.

Strawberry Shortcake
1 ½ oz. Amaretto
1 oz. Cream
2 oz. Fresh or Frozen Strawberries
1 scoop Vanilla Ice Cream

Combine all ingredients in a blender with ½ scoop of ice. Process until smooth. Top with whipped cream and a cherry.

Strawberry Smash
1 oz. Bacardi Light Rum
1 oz. Wilderberry Schnapps
½ oz. Bacardi 151 Rum
1 oz. Sour Mix
3 oz. Fresh Strawberries
1 whole Ripe Banana

Combine all ingredients in a blender with a scoop of ice. Process until smooth.

Strawberry-Cranberry Frost
2 oz. Vodka
4 oz. Cranberry Juice
4 oz. Frozen Strawberries

Combine all ingredients in a blender with a scoop of ice. Process until smooth.

Strawdka
1 ½ oz. Vodka
3 oz. Cream
4 oz. Fresh Strawberries
1 tsp. Vanilla Extract

Combine all ingredients in a blender with a scoop of ice. Process until smooth.

Summer Breeze
¾ oz. Creme de Banana
1 ¼ oz. Rum
3 oz. Orange Juice
1 ½ oz. Pineapple Juice

Combine all ingredients in a blender with a scoop of ice. Process until smooth. Garnish with an orange slice.

Summer Citrus Freeze
1 oz. Peach Schnapps
½ oz. Vodka
2 oz. Grapefruit Juice
2 oz. Fresh Strawberries

Combine all ingredients in a blender with a scoop of ice. Process until smooth. Garnish with a fresh strawberry.

Summer Delight
1 oz. Creme de Banana
4 oz. Orange Juice
2 oz. Fresh Strawberries

Combine all ingredients in a blender with a scoop of ice. Process until smooth.

Summertime Sting
½ oz. Cointreau
½ oz. Grand Marnier
½ oz. Bacardi Light Rum
½ oz. Vodka
Dash of Bacardi 151 Rum

Combine all ingredients in a blender with ½ of a peeled lime, 3 orange segments, a grapefruit segment and a scoop of ice. Process until smooth.

Sunburn
¾ oz. Peppermint Schnapps
¾ oz. Malibu Rum
2 oz. Pina Colada Mix

Combine all ingredients in a blender with a scoop of ice. Process until smooth.

Sunset
1 ½ oz. Tequila
¼ oz. Lime Juice
¼ oz. Grenadine

Combine all ingredients in a blender with ½ scoop of ice. Process until smooth. Garnish with a lime slice.

Super Bowl Cocktail
1 ½ oz. Baileys Irish Cream
1 ½ oz. Frangelico
1 oz. Orange Juice
1 scoop Vanilla Ice Cream

Combine all ingredients in a blender. Process until smooth. Garnish with an Oreo cookie.

Super Bowl Orange Crush
1 ½ oz. Vodka
1 raw Egg
1 tsp. Vanilla Extract
1 tsp. Sugar
5 oz. Orange Juice

Combine all ingredients in a blender with a scoop of ice. Process until smooth.

Surf's Up
½ oz. Creme de Banana
½ oz. Light Creme de Cacao
5 oz. Pineapple Juice
1 oz. Cream

Combine all ingredients in a blender with a scoop of ice. Process until smooth. Garnish with an orange slice and a cherry.

Surfsider
¾ oz. Kahlua
¾ oz. Malibu Rum
1 oz. Pina Colada Mix
1 scoop Vanilla Ice Cream

Combine all ingredients in a blender. Process until smooth.

Swamp Water
1 oz. Chambord
1 oz. Blue Curacao
1 oz. Absolut Vodka
1 oz. Southern Comfort
1 oz. Bacardi 151 Rum
3 oz. Orange Juice

Combine all ingredients in a blender with a scoop of ice. Process until smooth.

Sweet Dream
1 oz. Baileys Irish Cream
1 oz. Vodka
2 oz. Cream
1 ½ tsp. Powdered Sugar

Combine all ingredients in a blender with a scoop of ice. Process until smooth. Top with whipped cream.

Sweet Tart
2 oz. Vodka
3 oz. Cranberry Juice
3 oz. Pineapple Juice
Dash of Lime Juice

Combine all ingredients in a blender with a scoop of ice. Process until smooth. Garnish with a lime wheel.

Sweetie Baby
2 oz. Amaretto
2 scoops Vanilla Ice Cream

Combine both ingredients in a blender. Process until smooth. Top with toasted crushed almonds.

Swimming to the Shore by the Song of the Sunrise
1 oz. Gin
1 oz. Vodka
1 oz. Light Rum
1 oz. Tequila
3 oz. Pineapple Juice

Combine all ingredients in a blender with a scoop of ice. Process until smooth.

Taboo
1 oz. Light Rum
1 oz. Vodka
¼ oz. Pineapple Juice
¼ oz. Lemon Juice
Dash of Simple Syrup

Combine all ingredients in a blender with ½ scoop of ice. Process until smooth.

Tan Russian
1 ½ oz. Kahlua
2 oz. Milk
2 scoops Vanilla Ice Cream

Combine all ingredients in a blender. Process until smooth.

Taste of the Islands
1 oz. Myer's Dark Rum
2 oz. Malibu Rum
1 whole Ripe Banana
2 oz. Cream

Combine all ingredients in a blender with a scoop of ice. Process until smooth.

Tennessee Waltz
1 ¼ oz. Peach Schnapps
2 oz. Pineapple Juice
1 oz. Passion Fruit Juice
1 scoop Vanilla Ice Cream

Combine all ingredients in a blender. Process until smooth. Top with whipped cream and a strawberry.

Tequila Colada
1 oz. Tequila
1 ½ oz. Coco Lopez
2 oz. Pineapple Juice

Combine all ingredients in a blender with a scoop of ice. Process until smooth. Garnish with a pineapple chunk and a cherry.

Tequila Frost
1 ¼ oz. Tequila
1 ¼ oz. Pineapple Juice
1 ¼ oz. Grapefruit Juice
½ oz. Honey
½ oz. Grenadine
1 scoop Vanilla Ice Cream

Combine all ingredients in a blender. Process until smooth. Garnish with an orange slice and a cherry.

Terry
1 ½ oz. Tequila
1 ½ oz. Orange Juice
1 ½ oz. Pineapple Juice
½ oz. Coco Lopez

Combine all ingredients in a blender with a scoop of ice. Process until smooth.

Texas Sling
¾ oz. Amaretto
¾ oz. Coffee Liqueur
¾ oz. Baileys Irish Cream
¾ oz. Bacardi 151 Rum

Combine all ingredients in a blender with a scoop of ice. Process until smooth. Top with whipped cream.

These Nuts
¾ oz. Wild Turkey
¾ oz. Everclear
¾ oz. Baileys Irish Cream
¾ oz. Grenadine
¾ oz. Lime Juice

Combine all ingredients in a blender with a scoop of ice. Process until smooth.

Thurston Howell
¾ oz. Captain Morgan Spiced Rum
½ oz. Creme de Banana
2 oz. Orange Juice
1 oz. Sour Mix
½ oz. Simple Syrup

Combine all ingredients in a blender with a scoop of ice. Process until smooth. Float ½ oz. grenadine on top. Gently stir.

Tidal Wave
1 ¼ oz. Melon Liqueur
1 oz. Pineapple Juice
1 oz. Orange Juice
½ oz. Coco Lopez
1 ½ oz. Sour Mix
½ oz. Light Rum

Combine all ingredients in a blender with a scoop of ice. Process until smooth. Garnish

Tidbit
1 oz. Gin
¼ oz. Dry Sack Sherry
1 scoop Vanilla Ice Cream

Combine all ingredients in a blender. Process until smooth.

Tiger Tail
1 ¾ oz. Tuaca
½ oz. Triple Sec
2 oz. Orange Juice

Combine all ingredients in a blender with a scoop of ice. Process until smooth. Slowly pour ½ oz. Grenadine around the inside of a hurricane glass, then add frozen drink.

Tire Swing
1 ½ oz. Amaretto
1 oz. Bacardi 151 Rum
2 oz. Orange Juice

Combine all ingredients in a blender with a scoop of ice. Process until smooth. Garnish with a cherry.

Titanic Monkey
1 ½ oz. Creme de Banana
½ oz. Light Rum
½ oz. Vodka
2 oz. Pineapple Juice
2 oz. Coco Lopez

Combine all ingredients in a blender with a scoop of ice. Process until smooth.

Toasty Almond Colada
¾ oz. Amaretto
¾ oz. Kahlua
2 oz. Pina Colada Mix
1 scoop Vanilla Ice Cream

Combine all ingredients in a blender. Process until smooth.

Top Ten
1 ¼ oz. Captain Morgan Spiced Rum
1 oz. Coco Lopez
2 oz. Cola
1 oz. Cream

Combine all ingredients in a blender with a scoop of ice. Process until smooth.

Touchy Feely
1 ½ oz. Light Rum
½ oz. Brandy
¼ oz. Passion Fruit Syrup
¼ oz. Lemon Juice

Combine all ingredients in a blender with ½ scoop of ice. Process until smooth. Serve in a champagne flute.

Towson Dream
1 oz. Orange Curacao
1 oz. Triple Sec
2 oz. Orange Juice
2 scoops Vanilla Ice Cream

Combine all ingredients in a blender. Process until smooth.

Trade Winds
2 oz. Light Rum
½ oz. Sloe Gin
½ oz. Lime Juice
2 tsp. Sugar

Combine all ingredients in a blender with a scoop of ice. Process until smooth.

Trip to Paradise
¾ oz. Southern Comfort
¾ oz. Orange Juice
1 ½ oz. Pina Colada Mix

Combine all ingredients in a blender with a scoop of ice. Process until smooth.

Trolley Car
1 ¼ oz. Amaretto
2 oz. Fresh Strawberries
2 scoops Vanilla Ice Cream

Combine all ingredients in a blender. Process until smooth. Garnish with a strawberry.

Tropic Freeze
1 ¼ oz. Captain Morgan Spiced Rum
2 oz. Orange Juice
2 oz. Pineapple Juice
1 ½ oz. Coco Lopez
½ oz. Grenadine

Combine all ingredients in a blender with a scoop of ice. Process until smooth. Garnish with a pineapple slice and a cherry.

Tropical Blend
1 ¼ oz. Melon Liqueur
1 oz. Creme de Banana
2 oz. Pina Colada Mix

Combine all ingredients in a blender with a scoop of ice. Process until smooth.

Tropical Breeze
1 ¼ oz. Malibu Rum
1 ¼ oz. Creme de Banana
2 oz. Pina Colada Mix

Combine all ingredients in a blender with a scoop of ice. Process until smooth.

Tropical Freeze
2 oz. Finlandia Arctic Cranberry Vodka
¼ cup Peeled & Chopped Mango
½ cup Pineapple

Combine all ingredients in a blender with a scoop of ice. Process until smooth. Garnish with frozen cranberries and a pineapple slice.

Tropical Hooter
¾ oz. Malibu Rum
¾ oz. Melon Liqueur
¾ oz. Cranberry Juice
2 oz. Pina Colada Mix

Combine all ingredients in a blender with a scoop of ice. Process until smooth.

Tropical Madness
2 oz. Papaya Juice
1 oz. Pineapple Juice
½ oz. Grenadine
1 oz. Sour Mix
½ of a Ripe Banana
1 Lime Wedge

Combine all ingredients in a blender with a scoop of ice. Process until smooth. Garnish with a pineapple slice and a cherry.

Tropical Orange Crush
1 ¼ oz. Amaretto
1 ½ oz. Orange Juice
1 ½ oz. Pineapple Juice
Splash of Lemon Juice

Combine all ingredients in a blender with a scoop of ice. Process until smooth. Garnish with a pineapple slice.

Tropical Paradise
1 ¼ oz. Captain Morgan Spiced Rum
2 oz. Orange Juice
2 oz. Coco Lopez
¼ oz. Grenadine
½ of a Ripe Banana

Combine all ingredients in a blender with a scoop of ice. Process until smooth. Garnish with a pineapple slice and a cherry.

Tropical Storm
1 oz. Rum
½ oz. Creme de Banana
2 oz. Orange Juice
Splash of Pineapple Juice
Dash of Grenadine
1 Ripe Banana

Combine all ingredients in a blender with a scoop of ice. Process until smooth. Garnish with a pineapple slice.

Tropina Banana Daiquiri
1 ½ oz. Tropina
½ oz. Creme de Banana
¼ oz. Lime Juice
½ of a Ripe Banana
1 tsp. Sugar

Combine all ingredients in a blender with a scoop of ice. Process until smooth.

Tropina Peaches & Cream
1 ½ oz. Tropina
½ of a Ripe Peach
1 oz. Cream
1 scoop Vanilla Ice Cream

Combine all ingredients in a blender with ½ scoop of ice. Process until smooth.

Tropina Strawberry Daiquiri
1 ½ oz. Tropina
1 oz. Strawberry Liqueur
¼ oz. Lime Juice
1 tsp. Sugar
2 Strawberries

Combine all ingredients in a blender with a scoop of ice. Process until smooth. Garnish with a fresh strawberry.

Tuacaccino Freeze
1 ¼ oz. Tuaca
2 oz. Cold Cappuccino

Combine both ingredients in a blender with ½ scoop of ice. Process until smooth.

Tuitti-Fruitti
¾ oz. Rum
¾ oz. Strawberry Schnapps
¾ oz. Peach Schnapps
¾ oz. Creme de Banana

Combine all ingredients in a blender with a scoop of ice. Process until smooth.

Turkey Daiquiri
1 ½ oz. Wild Turkey
½ oz. Peach Schnapps
2 oz. Fresh Strawberries
1 whole Peach (pitted)
1 tbs. Brown Sugar
2 oz. Peach Juice

Combine all ingredients in a blender with a scoop of ice. Process until smooth. Garnish with a slice of fresh peach.

Ugly Mutha
¾ oz. Chambord
¾ oz. Blue Curacao
¾ oz. Absolut Vodka
¾ oz. Malibu Rum
¾ oz. Southern Comfort
2 oz. Orange Juice

Combine all ingredients in a blender with a scoop of ice. Process until smooth.

Up The Duff
½ oz. Brandy
½ oz. Coffee Liqueur
½ oz. Light Creme de Cacao
½ oz. Cream

2 scoops Vanilla Ice Cream
Combine all ingredients in a blender. Process until smooth.

Utopia 7
2 oz. Smirnoff Vodka
½ of a Ripe Banana
3 oz. Fresh Raspberries
2 scoops Strawberry Ice Cream

Combine all ingredients in a blender. Process until smooth.

Vanilla Shake
1 ½ oz. Licor 43
1 oz. Cream
1 raw Egg
1 scoop Vanilla Ice Cream

Combine all ingredients in a blender. Process until smooth. Top with whipped cream and a cherry.

Vanillaberry Shocker
1 oz. Bourbon
1 oz. Brandy
1 oz. Raspberry Syrup
1 tsp. Vanilla Extract
3 oz. Club Soda

Combine all ingredients in a blender with a scoop of ice. Process until smooth.

Velvet Hammer
¾ oz. Brandy
¾ oz. Triple Sec
¾ oz. Light Creme de Cacao
2 scoops Vanilla Ice Cream

Combine all ingredients in a blender. Process until smooth.

Viper's Venom
1 oz. Cinnamon Schnapps
1 oz. White Sambuca
1 oz. Peach Schnapps
2 scoops Vanilla Ice Cream

Combine all ingredients in a blender. Process until smooth.

Vodka Frosted Orange
2 oz. Vodka
2 oz. Orange Juice
2 scoops Vanilla Ice Cream

Combine all ingredients in a blender. Process until smooth.

Waist Coat Pocket
½ oz. Kahlua
½ oz. Amaretto
½ oz. Chocolate Schnapps
2 scoops Vanilla Ice Cream

Combine all ingredients in a blender. Process until smooth.

Wet Willy
2 oz. Vodka
3 oz. 7-Up
3 oz. Margarita Mix

Combine all ingredients in a blender with a scoop of ice. Process until smooth.

When Hell Freezes Over
¾ oz. Cinnamon Schnapps
¾ oz. Creme de Banana
2 oz. Orange Juice
2 oz. Cranberry Juice

Combine all ingredients in a blender with a scoop of ice. Process until smooth.

Whiskey Beer Sour
2 oz. Whiskey
4 oz. Lemonade
4 oz. Draft Beer

Combine all ingredients in a blender with a scoop of ice. Process until smooth. Pour into a beer mug.

Whiskey Slush
2 oz. Whiskey
3 oz. Unsweetened Iced Tea
2 oz. Orange Juice
2 oz. Lemonade
1 tbs. Sugar

Combine all ingredients in a blender with a scoop of ice. Process until smooth. Pour into a beer mug.

Whisper
¾ oz. Kahlua
¾ oz. Light Creme de Cacao
¾ oz. Brandy
1 scoop Vanilla Ice Cream

Combine all ingredients in a blender. Process until smooth.

White Cargo
1 oz. Gin
½ oz. White Wine
½ oz. Maraschino Liqueur
1 scoop Vanilla Ice Cream

Combine all ingredients in a blender. Process until smooth.

White Chocolate Raspberry Truffle
½ oz. Godet White Chocolate Liqueur
½ oz. Amaretto
½ oz. Chambord
½ oz. Creme de Curacao
2 oz. Cream
2 scoops Vanilla Ice Cream

Combine all ingredients in a blender. Process until smooth. Top with a sprinkle of cocoa

White Mexican
2 oz. Tequila
1 oz. Lime Juice
2 oz. Cream

Combine all ingredients in a blender with a scoop of ice. Process until smooth. Pour into a salt-rimmed cocktail glass.

White Mountain
2 oz. Sake
2 oz. Cream
1 ½ oz. Pineapple Juice
½ oz. Coco Lopez

Combine all ingredients in a blender with a scoop of ice. Process until smooth. Pour into a salt-rimmed cocktail glass.

White Velvet
1 ½ oz. White Sambuca
1 Egg White
1 tsp. Lemon Juice

Combine all ingredients in a blender with ½ scoop of ice. Process until smooth.

Wild Banshee
1 oz. Captain Morgan Spiced Rum
¼ oz. Amaretto
1 ½ oz. Cream
½ of a Ripe Banana

Combine all ingredients in a blender with a scoop of ice. Process until smooth.

Willy Wonka
1 ½ oz. Triple Sec
1 tsp. Vanilla Extract
½ oz. Chocolate Syrup
2 scoops Vanilla Ice Cream

Combine all ingredients in a
blender. Process until smooth.
Top with shaved chocolate.

Winter Sunshine
1 ½ oz. Light Rum
1 ½ oz. Vodka
3 oz. Orange Juice
1 whole Ripe Banana
1 tsp. Sugar

Combine all ingredients in a
blender with a scoop of ice.
Process until smooth.

Xylophone
1 oz. Tequila
½ oz. Light Creme de Cacao
½ oz. Simple Syrup
1 oz. Cream

Combine all ingredients in a
blender with ½ scoop of ice.
Process until smooth.

Yellow Bird
½ oz. Myer's Dark Rum
¼ oz. Galliano
½ oz. Creme de Banana
2 oz. Pineapple Juice

Combine all ingredients in a
blender with a scoop of ice.
Process until smooth. Garnish
with a pineapple slice and a
cherry.

Yellow Strawberry
1 oz. Rum
1 oz. Creme de Banana
½ oz. Sour Mix
2 oz. Fresh or Frozen
Strawberries
½ of a Ripe Banana

Combine all ingredients in a
blender with a scoop of ice.
Process until smooth.

Yellow Tiger
1 ½ oz. Absolut Citron Vodka
2 oz. Lemonade
2 scoops Lemon Sherbet

Combine all ingredients in a
blender. Process until smooth.

Yumdinger
¾ oz. Amaretto
¾ oz. Cognac
1 scoop Haagen-Dazs Rum
Raisin Ice Cream
1 oz. Club Soda

Combine all ingredients in a
blender. Process until smooth.

Zafter Zock
1 ½ oz. After Shock
Cinnamon Liqueur
4 oz. Zima

Combine both ingredients in a
blender with a scoop of ice.
Process until smooth.

Zodiac
1 ½ oz. Light Rum
1 oz. Triple Sec
½ oz. Creme de Banana
2 oz. Lemon Juice
2 oz. Orange Juice
Dash of Grenadine

Combine all ingredients in a
blender with a scoop of ice.
Process until smooth.

NOTES & MY RECIPES

NOTES & MY RECIPES

Made in the USA
Columbia, SC
06 April 2023

14953220R00048